ALASKA

BY

MOTORCYCLE

by

Dr. Gregory W. Frazier

PUBLISHED BY:

Arrowstar Publishing
P.O. Box 100134
Denver, Colorado 80250-0134

ALASKA

BY

MOTORCYCLE

BY DR. GREGORY W. FRAZIER

Published By:

Arrowstar Publishing
P.O. 100134
Denver, Colorado 80250-0134

copyright © 2006 by Dr. Gregory W. Frazier
First Printing 1996
Printed in the United States of America
Third Edition

Library of Congress Cataloging in Publication Data:

Frazier, Dr. Gregory W.
  Alaska by Motorcycle

  1.   Motorcycles — Alaska
  II.   Title
ISBN 0-935151-48-6

Warning - Disclaimer

This book is designed to provide information in regard to the subject matter covered. It is not the purpose of this book to reprint all the information that is otherwise available to the user, but to complement, amplify and supplement other sources.

Every effort has been made to make this book as complete and as accurate as possible. However, there may be mistakes both typographical and in content. This book contains information obtained and verified on a best efforts basis only up to the printing date.

The purpose of this book is to educate and inform. Arrowstar Publishing, its agents and assigns, publisher or author shall have neither liability nor responsibility to any person or entity with respect to any loss or damage caused or alleged to be caused directly or indirectly by the information contained in this book.

Any correspondence concerning the contents of this book, including revisions or additions, should be directed to Publisher, Arrowstar Publishing, c/o Alaska by Motorcycle, P.O. Box 100134, Denver, CO 80250-0134.

Warning - Disclaimer

DEDICATION

In memory of Thomas Schmidt (November 23, 1958 - July 14, 1990) of Betzweiler-Walde in the Black Forest, Germany. Thomas was my motorcycling pal.

He returned from his motorcycle adventure in Alaska with a smile bigger than Alaska itself. I am happy to have shared some of his motorcycling adventure through life.

TABLE OF CONTENTS

Special thanks to Jean M. Turk, Word Processor,
for the fine work on the maps and
manuscript preparation.

INTRODUCTION

When I first went to Alaska the horror stories of the "Alcan" Highway were true. Broken windshields, mud ruts, no gas, bears, dust, and hundreds of miles of gravel road were what was found.

Each year things got better on the what is now called The Alaska Highway. Today the entire 1,400-mile section from Mile Post -0- in Dawson Creek to Delta Junction is paved, except for those sections being repaired. In fact, much of the original Alcan Highway no longer exists. The new Alaska Highway runs parallel to much of the old Alcan which sometimes can be seen running through the woods.

Today any vehicle can drive the Alaska Highway to Alaska. In July riders can often see a convoy of Airstream trailers being pulled to or from Anchorage as they clog the road. Motorcycles of every size and shape journey to Alaska and the Arctic Circle, from 250 cc dirt bikes to 1600 cc Gold-wings. Sidecars, trailers, tricycles and even relics from the past like Indians all make the journey.

My advice to any motorcyclists wanting to venture North To Alaska is not to worry about the horror stories—just get on your motorcycle and ride to Alaska. However, just like preparing for any long trip, prepare both yourself and your motorcycle. From Seattle to Anchorage and return is nearly 5,000 miles, much of it uninhabited. Prepared adventurers to Alaska experience motorcycle riding like none other in the world, a true adventure of a lifetime.

I have traveled all over the world by motorcycle and still find riding to Alaska an unparalleled experience.

CHAPTER 1

WHAT MOTORCYCLE TO TAKE?

Any kind of motorcycle can be ridden to Alaska, and probably has been. From Seattle, Washington, to Anchorage, Alaska, is approximately 2,400 miles, all of which can be ridden over paved roads so any motorcycle someone can sit atop for that distance can be ridden.

If the motorcyclist wants to take some model that is less comfortable, for instance a "chopped model," and they are not looking forward to sitting astride 1200 cc's of a vibrating washing machine loaded with bowling balls, they can load the motorcycle on the ferryboat just north of Seattle at Bellingham and ride the boat to Haines, Alaska. From there it is only 775 miles to Anchorage.

On the other hand, if the motorcyclist is more adventuresome, they can ride their motorcycle over nearly 1,000 miles of gravel roads to Anchorage. Oftentimes if it has rained, these gravel roads turn into mud wallows and become very slippery, and a test even for the more skilled riders. Therefore, a dual-purpose machine may be the rider's choice.

Each summer all types of motorcycles travel north. Some pull trailers, others have sidecars, and occasionally some have both. Once I met a fellow traveling from Alaska to Seattle on a 50 cc Honda who said he was doing it just to see if he could do it, which I expect he did. There was no reason he could not, unless he ran out of time due to his short travel days, about 200 miles each day.

(Top) German rider found this machine adequate for himself and companion for trip to Alaska, and then around the United States. (Bottom) Two German riders on their way to Alaska near Dease Lake, British Columbia. A $125.00 tire in the Lower 48 can cost $250.00 in Alaska or along the way, if one can be found. If you are on a budget, or unsure about finding what is needed for your motorcycle, it is better to carry what you will need.

Another time I met a rider from Los Angeles on a Suzuki GSXR 1000. He had stopped for gas near Whitehorse on his way back from Anchorage. For luggage all he carried was a sleeping bag wrapped in a plastic garbage sack tied to the rear of his seat. He explained that his vacation was only seven days long and he had wanted to see Alaska. He was averaging approximately 1,000 miles per day and fully expected to be back to work on the following Monday. While he was able to ride to and from Alaska on the Suzuki, he did acknowledge that his bottom was sore and his back felt as if he had been broken in half. The most vivid memory I have of him is the thousands of mosquitoes and flies plastered to his fairing and helmet, which he had not bothered to wash off. In places they could have been scraped off with a shovel.

Whatever type of motorcycle is being contemplated for the ride north, the main consideration should be comfort. The rider can expect rain in July, and sometimes snow. It is not unusual for it to rain or be overcast the entire trip to and from Alaska. Weather protection in the form of a windshield or fairing is strongly recommended. Additionally, these "wind pushers" also serve to stop flying stones launched by cars or trucks approaching or passing. While the highway up and back is paved, there are long stretches that are under repair or being resurfaced constantly. A common road surface of "chip seal," or small stones sometimes nearly the size of marbles, is widely used, and these stones are easily lofted by passing vehicles. It is comforting to hear one of them hit the windshield or fairing of the motorcycle, knowing that had it not been between the rider and the stone the contact point could have been a knee or neck.

The second comfort factor should be the motorcycle seat. Select a motorcycle that is comfortable to sit on all day. If the bike has a sport seat or something akin to a board, the owner might want to purchase an aftermarket touring replacement. If the rider chooses to keep their stock seat and it is a "cheek buster," they might want to condition themselves before leaving

5

(**Top**) German motorcyclist, having been to the end of the roads in Alaska, is seen here as he heads south to a BMW motorcycle rally in the Lower 48. Motorcycle was shipped to the United States from Germany, a common practice with European travelers encountered in the far north. (**Bottom**) German traveler, camping his way to Alaska, seen here south of Dawson, Yukon.

by having their buddy whack them on the back end with a two-by-four every day for a month before departure. Because of the long distances between motels or campgrounds, it is not uncommon to ride 400-500 miles each day. Sitting on an uncomfortable bench can make long days torturous.

While pulling a trailer behind a motorcycle may allow the driver to carry more gear or shift weight off the motorcycle, motorcycling to Alaska is not like driving down an interstate highway. The Alaska Highway is extremely rough in places, with deep, soft gravel in construction areas and slippery, oil-covered hardpan in others. Ruts are not uncommon in some of the older sections and frost heaves, especially between Haines Junction and the Alaska border, cause even the solo machine to sway. Several of the people I have met over the years pulling trailers behind their bikes had stories to recount about crashes caused by road conditions. One of these ended up shipping the whole rig back to the states from Anchorage, as he crashed twice on the way up and his wife broke her leg in the second fall. Another trailer crasher I met went down when the change from macadam to gravel was unmarked and he hit the marbles at 70 miles per hour and went sideways, before flipping the trailer and highsiding himself off the motorcycle. The custom matching paint on his Goldwing and trailer had custom matching scratches and he made the rest of the trip without his windshield, CB or AM/FM radio.

I am not a fan of trailers attached to motorcycles, but I realize some people pull them for necessary reasons. One of my friends pulls his so he has somewhere to put the stuff he and his wife buy along the way. Tee shirts, wall clocks, snow domes, and bargains at garage sales all go into the trailer as they travel. Having pulled his trailer behind his Harley from Seattle to Anchorage and exhausted himself doing so, he detached the trailer and sent it home to Los Angeles via air cargo, and thereafter he and his wife made daily stops at packaging stores or had souvenirs shipped home along the route back to the "Lower 48."

7

(**Top**) From Florida to the Arctic Circle and return, this BMW K75S did the job. (**Bottom**) Motorcyclists with various brands and models collect in campground near Fairbanks, Alaska, to compare routes, road conditions, and machines. Photo taken at 10:00 p.m. in July, still light enough not to need a flash.

8

Sidecars offer an equal challenge to the pilot, as do trailers, although I am only aware of two sidecars being shipped home from Alaska. The biggest challenge for the sidecar driver are the ruts in the road which cause the rig to move back and forth across the driving lane. The ruts are spaced farther apart than the wheels of the sidecar rig, and with the many turns in the road, the driver is constantly fighting the rig as either one wheel or the other tries to ride up one of the ruts. Even for a two-wheel rider, these sections of road can be tiring. For the sidecar driver they can be exhausting.

I have often been questioned about my sanity when people find out I drive a motorcycle to Alaska (always by car drivers). However, even I have to question the sanity of anyone who would want to make the trip with a sidecar pulling a trailer. That is not to say it cannot be done. It can. Anything can be driven or ridden to Alaska. People do it on bicycles. Others pull Airstream trailers behind the family station wagon. Semi trucks do it year-round, and I once talked to a man doing it on cross-country skis mounted on small wheels. I would not be surprised seeing someone make the trip on a unicycle in a clown outfit. But pulling a sidecar with a trailer attached? I would suggest loading it on the boat in Bellingham, Washington, and watching whales for a couple of days while floating to Haines, Alaska. Once there, the rider will have plenty of riding time to enjoy their rig in Alaska, and they can purchase a bumper sticker along the way that says, "I TRAVELED THE ALASKA HIGHWAY," which they will have done . . . from Haines Junction to at least Tok, Alaska. No one will know the difference, and the driver's life will be less filled with terror.

Whatever model or size of motorcycle the Alaska traveler decides to take, it should be in very good mechanical condition. Anchorage and Fairbanks have motorcycle dealers and repair shops, but there are long stretches between the Lower 48 and Alaska where a breakdown can be very expensive. First, the machine may have to be collected and hauled into the

(**Top**) Collection of riders leaving Seattle, Washington. Fifteen-day, 5,500-mile round trip. (**Bottom**) Near the Arctic Circle in Alaska. Which one is the American rider? BMW in the middle. Left is from Germany. Right is from Switzerland.

next major town, at $5.00 per mile. If repairs can be made in the next town, expect parts and labor to be expensive, very expensive. If major parts are needed for repairs, they often must be shipped from the Lower 48, sometimes taking up to a week.

My advice is take what you think you might need. If your motorcycle is one of those famous for needing a stator, you may want to carry an extra. The added weight is nothing compared to a five-day stay in a $125.00 per night motel, $75.00 - $100.00 per hour labor costs and paying twice what the part would cost at home.

If an oil change or some other routine maintenance is going to be needed during the trip, consider doing it yourself. Not only are costs high once you cross into Canada and Alaska, but scheduling is a problem. I have been told by motorcycle dealers and repair shops in Alaska that as a tourist you take second position on work schedules to locals. This is because the local motorcyclist lives in the area and supports the shop all year round. As a tourist you are only passing through and are not expected back.

Additionally, tourists often expect a motorcycle dealer to stop scheduled work on local customers' motorcycles to attend to the tourist's problem, which is an unrealistic expectation. Confrontations with dealers and service personnel have hardened some dealers to the point where your work may be the last they schedule. Fortunately, most motorcycle dealers along the route and in Alaska are sensitive to traveling motorcyclists, their travel schedules, and in some cases even their budgets, and try to get a broken tourist on the road as quickly as possible. I know of several dealers who have opened their businesses after hours and worked into the early morning to help a stranded traveler on their way. This is not to be expected, but it does happen. Remember, just because you ride a certain brand of motorcycle and they operate a dealership for that brand, you have no influence over their business. Write all the letters you want to "the company," make all the calls you

(Top) Harley Davidson from Tennessee to the Arctic Circle, Alaska, and return. **(Bottom)** Hand-built Harley Davidson made the trip—Indiana to Alaska and return.

can, nothing will get you on the road any faster than what schedule the dealer wants to assign to your problem.

I suggest that if you are going to need work done during your travels you call and schedule it a week or two in advance, especially during June, July and August. An option is take what you need and do the work yourself. Offer to pay a gas station for use of their bay and oil catch pan and oil disposal. An oil change at a shop can cost close to $100.00. Make a reasonable offer to a gas station and you can save $75.00 or more. Sometimes the gas station will not accept payment and even offer to help you, but they like being offered something for use of their facilities. Remember, from September through May their business is more than slow, often it is dead, and they close.

Any motorcycle can be ridden to Alaska. It should be in good running condition and it should be comfortable. A ferryboat ride up and back can reduce wear and tear on equipment and rider by taking 3,500 miles off the trip, but maintenance may still be needed. Be prepared and be patient. If you have to wait a few days, enjoy the area, because this is why you left the Lower 48, to see Alaska.

A NOTE ON TIRES: Due t your added weight and the "chip seal" used on the roads, expect faster than normal tire wear, as much as 200%!

(Top) Harley Davidson with trailer on the way to Alaska. These campers pulled the trailer over the Cassiar Highway through British Columbia when much of it was unpaved. **(Bottom)** Tennessee BMW pilot and wife logged over 12,000 miles on their trip to Alaska and return.

14

(Top) Tourist in campground watches motorcyclist do routine maintenance at the end of the day while saying, "I used to have a motorcycle . . . . ".
(Bottom) "Commander Bob" from Reading, Pennsylvania, has made the trip to Alaska twice with his Police Special Harley Davidson with sidecar. Asked if he would do it again, his response is, "In a minute!"

CHAPTER 2

TENT OR MOTEL?

Motels, lodges, roadhouses and cabins are plentiful along both highway routes to Alaska, but they can be expensive. In the Yukon one can expect to pay $100.00 per night for a room that would cost $30.00 per night in the Lower 48. A room in a lodge or roadhouse can be equally expensive. A single room in Fairbanks can easily cost $125.00 for the night.

During the summer months it is not uncommon for every room in a town along the Alaska Highway to be filled, having been reserved months in advance.

If the traveler is expecting four star accommodations along the road to Alaska, they are in for a surprise. While there are a number of nice hotels and motels on the way north, the general rule of thumb is to expect the worst and you will be pleasantly surprised with what you get. A black and white TV is quite acceptable in a motel room where the town has no TV reception.

For the motel traveler it is strongly recommended they make reservations several months in advance, particularly if they are traveling in July or August. A letter to the motel after making the reservation is also suggested, as changes in personnel and lost paperwork can leave a traveler with no room in a filled town and 200-300 miles to the next town of any size. While this is not common, it does happen.

Camping ranges from $5.00 per night to $15.00 per night. There are many public and private campgrounds along the routes north. Public campgrounds generally do not have electricity

(Top) A lodge offering rooms along the Alaska Highway. During the "high season," rooms can cost $75.00 per night. (Bottom) A group of motorcyclists discovered this clean, inexpensive motel in 100 Mile House, British Columbia. It has a campground in the back for those wanting to camp.

18

or showers. Some have free firewood as well as attendants who check you in. None of the public camping facilities take reservations. Some of the public camping facilities have well water and some offer sheltered kitchen areas (sleeping in these areas is not permitted).

Private camping facilities offer many more amenities. These include showers (some requiring quarters to activate hot water for a period of time), laundries, stores, telephones, and all will accept reservations. Some will agree to receive parcels mailed or shipped to you prior to your arrival, parcels like tires. The cost for private campgrounds is usually a little higher than public camping, but not always.

Some private campgrounds do not accept tent campers. These campgrounds cater to the motorhome travelers, and are not "biker friendly." The reason is merely economic. A motorhome space will rent out for $30.00 to $50.00 per night, while a tent camper is usually willing to pay only $10.00 to $20.00.

If camping is the choice of the traveler for June, July or August, it is best to call ahead for reservations much the same as you would for a motel, as sometimes the campgrounds are full. When calling, make sure they accept motorcycles. Another question to ask is if you must leave your motorcycle at a common parking area and carry your gear to your tent site.

In Canada, camping in rest areas or turnouts is illegal unless otherwise posted. It can also be unsafe, particularly in the far north, as trash cans located in these areas attract bears. Bears find camper food much to their liking, so if you are considering camping away from designated campgrounds, "Beware of Bears!"

Leaving Whitehorse one evening, I saw a bicyclist setting up his camp in the woods to the side of the road just outside of town. As I drove by, I suspected he was trying to save money as there were several very nice campgrounds only a few miles back. About 100 yards past his camping site, unknown to him,

(**Top**) An upscale motel along the Alaska Highway. (**Bottom**) A dormitory style motel along the Alaska Highway.

I passed the entrance to the city dump, the evening buffet for bears. I have often wondered how much sleep the bicyclist got that night with all the noise and traffic (four-legged) so near his tent.

On another occasion, one of my traveling partners broke down about 150 miles from Watson Lake on the Campbell Highway, a gravel road. As it was late in the day when his motorcycle died, and pulling him was impossible because of our combined traveling gear, we decided he would camp near a bridge for the night while I rode to town for assistance. I left him a can of spaghetti and a couple of candy bars while I went on to Watson Lake for a nice shower and steak dinner, promising to return early next morning with a pickup truck.

Upon returning next morning, we spied my traveling partner high in the fir trees next to the bridge, where he had spent the night. It seems that sometime in the early evening a mother bear and her two cubs wandered into his camp and liked his camp so much they stayed for the night. In the morning they left shortly before we arrived, but our tree dweller chose to stay where he was versus returning to his destroyed campsite. The bears had also pushed over his motorcycle while rummaging through his saddlebags for food, which caused all the gas to run out, but since he was riding his Harley back to town in the pickup it did not matter to him. What did matter to him was the fact that the bears ripped his custom seat to shreds. It had been a bad night for the biker and a fun night for the bears.

Bears are not the only problem for campers. Moose can be a much bigger problem for someone in a tent. One of my fellow campers suffered the great indignity of being taken to the hospital after a moose walked on his small, one-man tent and stepped on his groin. It seems that a moose cannot tell the difference between a thick bush, which they easily walk through, and a tent the same size. My biker friend was lying on his back listening to his tape player with earphones when the moose stepped on him.

21

(Top) After two days of camping in public campgrounds with no showers, this motorcyclist decided to brave the cold of a lake in the Yukon. Here he fights off mosquitoes. (Bottom) Campground life can cost as little as $5.00 per night. Your motorcycle rests next to you.

Motorcyclist campers are cautioned not to leave anything leather outside their tents at night. Many animals like leather boots, jackets, gloves and billfolds, all of which have been known to disappear overnight. Tankbags with food inside are also visited by uninvited four-legged guests, some of whom can easily put their paws on a gas tank while chewing through the strongest gortex or nylon straps.

For camping information or motel listings in Canada and Alaska, the best place to start is *The Milepost*. This 750-page publication is updated annually and contains a wealth of information, including maps, ferry schedules, campgrounds, motels, and general tourist information. It is an absolute must for the northbound traveler. At $25.95, it is the best bargain north of the Canadian border.

The Milepost
1-800-726-4707
www.themilepost.com

(Top) Public campground in the Yukon. Unattended, it was $5.00 for the night, had free firewood and fresh well water. No shower or motorhomes. (Bottom) Australian motojournalist relishes "green soft grass" for pitching his tent. At home he camps in the "Outback" on red sand.

(**Top**) Swiss camper who looks as if she is enjoying camping on her way to Alaska. (**Bottom**) Australian motorcycle camper taking souvenir photographs of campground wildlife, here a tethered Keeshond dog, near Fairbanks, Alaska.

(**Top**) Free camping along the Alaska Highway. Not recommended except for the most hardened traveler. These cabins have many visitors at night. (**Bottom**) One of the visitors to the above cabin. On the next trip to Alaska I let the bear have the cabin for the night while I paid to stay in a campground. The night cost more money, but I got more sleep.

The best source for motorcycle travelers' information on travel to and from Canada from others who have "been there, done that" can be found at:
www.horizonsunlimited.com
As the ad says: "Don't leave home without it." Log on before you go, and sign up for their regular Ezine.

CHAPTER 3

RIDER'S CHECKLIST OF WHAT TO TAKE

This checklist has been developed over a number of years and specifically for the motorcyclist riding to Alaska. It takes into consideration travel through some very remote areas where regular motorcycle service centers are not available. It also assumes the motorcyclist can do some minor mechanical work on his/her equipment. The user of this list should adapt it to their own type of equipment and riding and not consider it complete as each rider will have their own special needs and wants. Therefore, this checklist is to be considered a guideline and not all inclusive.

ALASKA RIDER'S CHECKLIST

(1)   Riding Gear:

        Helmet
        Riding jacket/pants
        Riding boots
        Light leather riding gloves
        Heavy (warm) leather riding gloves
        Rain jacket
        Rain pants
        Rain boots
        Thermal top
        Thermal bottom

It is not unusual for a business listed on my maps or in other publications to "go out of business" over the winter. Once, when stopping for gas in Ross River, Yukon, I asked about the next gas station and how late it would be open, as it was approaching four in the afternoon and I knew it to be nearly 150 miles down the road. I was informed it had closed and I would have to make it to Watson Lake on however much gas I could carry. I changed my riding style to a conservative 50 miles per hour and filled an empty milk container from the nearby trash can with an extra gallon, which got me to Watson Lake on fumes. If your motorcycle is equipped with a small gas tank, you may want to change to a larger one before entering Canada or purchase a gas can for those times when you might be "cutting it close" from gas station to gas station.

Scarf/bandanna

Riding conditions vary considerably. The rider can expect 115° temperatures to possible snow conditions at the higher altitudes of the Rocky Mountains. There will also be rain, and in some cases, cold rain. Remember that the permafrost does not melt in Alaska and the Yukon. This is where the rider will find very cool riding conditions, especially when it rains.

Optional safety gear, like back protectors, is highly recommended.

Other Riding Gear:

_____

_____

_____

(2)   Clothing:

Underclothing (4 days)
Socks (4 pair—2 warm)
Sweatshirt/sweater
2 pairs of pants/jeans
Jacket (for evening wear when your riding equipment
    might be wet/cold)
Walking shoes
Handkerchiefs
Bathing suit
Bath towel
Shirts (for wearing with riding gear—long-sleeve type)

A "mini-mart" of the north, these "one-stop" gas stations/cafes offer interesting rest stops after long stretches of highway. Gas, unleaded regular and premium, is available well within the reach of most motorcycle gas tanks.

Not considered are any "dress-up" affairs. All restaurants have very informal dress codes and therefore the rider can plan on bringing comfortable clothing. Many campgrounds have laundry facilities in them.

Other Clothing:

_____

_____

_____

(3)   Sleeping Equipment (Camping)

Waterproof tent
Warm sleeping bag
Air mattress/sleeping pad

Some hints: Get some good, heavy-duty tent pegs for your tent. The ground can be very hard (rocks) in some places. An air mattress/sleeping pad can be bulky, but remember that you will be sleeping on the ground. This will be only a few feet above the permafrost in some cases. Some riders also carry a large plastic sheet to throw over their tent in the rain. These are inexpensive and can also be used for a ground cloth or a cover for the motorcycle. Other riders also carry a small hammer for their tent pegs . . . it can save time. The hammers that are also a small ax seem to be especially useful.

Cash is king along the Alaska Highway. Many roadhouses, gas stations and cafes do not accept credit cards. Travelers checks are nearly always accepted. Oftentimes businesses are only open for the summer traffic.

Other Sleeping Equipment:

_____

_____

_____

(4)   Motorcycle Tools/Spare Parts

Good tool kit
Tire pressure gauge
Tire pump, Instant Air
Tire repair kit
Tire irons/bead breaker
Spare front/rear tube
Master link/chain breaker
Mixed nut/bolt/washer kit
Chain lube
Small duct tape
Epoxy glue (optional)
Spare sparkplug(s)
Spare points
Gas line
Spare set of motorcycle keys
Clutch cable
Fuses
Electrical wire/tape
Plastic headlight cover

For those of you who have motorcycles famous for eating stators, rotors, CDIs or other electrical parts, it is recommended that you carry a spare of what you might need. Once across the border, you will not find much in the way of spare parts, even when you find a motorcycle

(Top) If you have a heavy motorcycle prone to falling over, you may want to carry a winch, or travel with several friends. **(Bottom)** Waterproof boots are a must because of the chances of rain, or stream crossings.

36

repair shop. From Prince George, B.C., to Anchorage, you are pretty much on your own. You may want to call the dealers up there to see if they will hold what you do not want to carry (tires).

Other Spare Equipment:

_____

_____

_____

(5) <u>Cooking Gear (Camping)</u>:

Burner/small stove
Cooking kit
Can opener
Knife/fork/spoon
Dish rag/scraper
Dish soap
Sharp knife
Canteen/water container
Plastic drinking/coffee cup
Matches/lighter

Cooking is optional. Restaurants are available all along the route, however, not always close to campgrounds. If you are going to cook, you may not want to do it for all meals. In many cases, you will find that our American campgrounds are not quite so nice as those we find in other countries . . . that is to say, they do not have fully equipped kitchens. You had better plan on bringing what you will need for cooking. Cooking stoves that run on gasoline are popular. You can drain the gas out of your

Mosquitoes peak in about June and are actively penetrating skin to nourish eggs well into the fall. They can bite through thin material, such as a cotton shirt, tight-fitting jeans and socks. They rely on their antennae to smell and are drawn to moisture, carbon dioxide, warmth and dark colors. A breeze of five miles per hour grounds most mosquitoes, so try to keep moving or put your tent where there is a slight breeze. Mosquito repellents containing diethyl-meta-toluamide (DEET) are the best for keeping mosquitoes away because it jams their sensors so they cannot tell if you are a meal. Other pests, like buffalo gnats and no-see-ums, also bite through light clothing like jeans. Wear leathers or other protective gear and apply a DEET repellent to unprotected areas during the day. At night, before retiring, spray the inside of your tent (or motel room) or burn a mosquito coil (not recommended by tent manufacturers) one-half hour before retiring.

motorcycle gas tank with your spare gas line and that way you will not find yourself carrying or looking for those bottles of propane.

Other Cooking Gear:

_____

_____

_____

(6)   Miscellaneous:

Multipurpose knife
Flashlight
Nylon rope
Plastic bags (for rain/dirty clothes)
Toilet kit
Camera/film
Lip balm
Sun protection lotion
Sunglasses
Writing supplies/notebook/diary
Bungee cords
Spare glasses/contacts
Small supply paper towels
Insect goop
First aid supplies
Tank bag
Maps
Medical card
Photocopy of all your documents (travelers checks, passport, driver's license, insurance card, prescriptions, vehicle registration, credit cards, etc.)

CAUTION
EXTREME - DANGER
YOU ARE ABOUT TO ENTER THE MOST
HAZARDOUS AREA IN THE U.S.
"OUR PUBLIC HIGHWAY SYSTEM"
- FASTEN YOUR SAFETY BELT -

Travel through Canada to Alaska can be just as risky as travel anywhere in the United States. Somewhere on your person you should carry medical information such as who to contact in case of emergency, any special medical requirements or allergies, and name of your insurance carrier. Before leaving the United States you should check with your insurance company to see if you will be covered while traveling through Canada. If not, you may want to purchase special travelers insurance.

One year a motorcyclist traveling between Whitehorse and Haines Junction suffered a heart attack and drove off the road and well into the trees. No one knew where he was or that he was missing. He was not discovered for three days. Animals had pretty well picked him clean. You may want to leave your itinerary with someone back home and arrange to check in once in a while.

$ — Travelers checks
Credit cards

Other Miscellaneous Equipment:

_____

_____

_____

While the above list might take up a trailer, I have gotten it easily onto one bike . . . you just have to be selective . . . and creative. Some of the items can be purchased along the way, while others can be left at home. This is a guide . . . use it accordingly.

(7)   Money:

Below is an estimate for funds necessary for a standard trip. For each rider this will vary. For instance, if the rider chooses to cook all meals rather than purchase them in restaurants, the cost will be lower. Or, if the rider chooses to spend some nights in a hotel/motel instead of staying in campgrounds, their costs will increase. Repair costs may be very expensive, depending on what is needed. One point to remember is that everything is more expensive in Canada and Alaska. In fact, everything is about two times as expensive, if it can be found. That part you paid $125.00 for in Ohio might cost you as much as $250.00 in the Yukon and take several days to be shipped in by air.

So, the following chart is just an estimate. Part of the fun is trying to make sure you plan well enough ahead of time to keep money in your pocket.

41

ESTIMATED TRIP EXPENSES		
Daily Expenses	Gas/Oil	$75.00
	Food	$35.00
	Total	**$110.00/day**
(_____ tour days x $110.00/day)		
Total Daily Expenses		**$**
Plus	Tire (s)	$
	Repairs	$
	Luxury Items	$
	Souvenirs	$
	Miscellaneous Items	$
	Motel/Camping Fee per night times # of nights _____	$
Grand Total Funds Required		**$**

ATM's are plentiful as you travel through Canada to Alaska. You should also plan on carrying cash or travelers checks. If you are a member of AAA, travelers checks, both in Canadian and United States dollars, are free. U.S. dollar travelers checks will be taken everywhere but the exchange rate you get may be less than you would get at a bank. The same is true if you use U.S. dollars.

Mastercard and VISA cards are accepted more often than American Express or other cards. Many restaurants, campgrounds and gas stations do not accept credit cards. Cash or travelers checks work everywhere. I have found that I do best if I carry Canadian travelers checks for use in Canada and pay for everything with them or cash. I lose a little when I have to convert U.S. dollars to Canadian dollars at the border or along the way. I try to estimate how much I will need in Canadian dollars before I go and get that amount in Canadian travelers checks from AAA before leaving, along with my free maps of Canada and Alaska.

WHAT NOT TO TAKE

I am guilty of carrying too much gear when I travel. On my trips to Alaska I have carried a fifty-foot length of rope I have yet to use. I also carry a hand-operated air pump for tire repairs, which has yet to be uncoupled from its resting place under my motorcycle seat. The one or two times I have had a flat tire I have used the can of Instant Air I carry and it has filled the tube enough to get me to a gas station. On my next trip I will probably still have both rope and tire pump. They make me feel better as I travel.

One traveler I met carried his collection of CDs in a large, heavy box. I asked him what he was going to do with them and he said he thought maybe he would find motels along the way that had CD players in the room. He wisely shipped them home upon arriving in Anchorage.

Canada does not permit entry of handguns. Leave them home or you will have to leave them at the border. Pepper spray is also prohibited. One of my riding partners felt he had to be armed to protect himself "from the bears," so carried a compound bow and arrows, which he used one night to shoot trees. The bow was legal but awkward, however, it may have served it purpose by scaring away all the bears along the route, as we saw not one in 6,000 miles.

CHAPTER 4

ENTERING CANADA

To get to Alaska by motorcycle you have to pass through Canada. Driving or taking the ferryboat makes no difference, you will have to pass through a Canadian customs/border crossing. For the citizen or permanent resident of the United States this usually presents little difficulty. For native born U.S. citizens, neither a passport or visa is required to enter Canada. However, to speed the time required for crossing, it is best to have some form of identification readily available in case the border officials request proof, which they do on occasion. Proof is usually:

(1)   A passport with photo.
(2)   Driver's license and voters registration (together).
(3)   Some employment cards with description and photo.

The Canadian government says that a social security card or driver's license alone are not considered positive identification.

For a naturalized U.S. citizen, a naturalization certificate is considered adequate proof. Resident Alien Cards (U.S. Form I-151 or Form I-551) are considered proof for permanent residents of the U.S. who are not U.S. citizens.

As a practical matter, border officials usually ask the tourist simple questions such as where they were born, mother's maiden name, or where they live. A simple and concise answer will often result in the motorcyclist being waved

Maps, brochures and travel-related questions on Canada. Contact:

ALBERTA: Travel Alberta
10155 102 St., 3rd Floor
Edmonton, AB T5J 4L6 Canada
Tele. # (800) 661-8888

BRITISH Tourism British Columbia
COLUMBIA: Parliament Buildings
Victoria, BC V8V 1X4 Canada
Tele. # (800) 663-6000

NORTHWEST Dept. of Economic Development & Tourism
TERRITORIES: Tourism Development & Marketing
Box 1320
Yellowknife, NT X1A 2L9 Canada
Tele. # (800) 661-0788

YUKON Tourism Yukon
TERRITORY: Box 2703
Whitehorse, YT Y1A 2C6 Canada
Tele. # (403) 667-5340

46

through. Sometimes the officials will ask where the motorcyclist is going, how long they plan on being in Canada, and whether they will be working while in Canada. Usually, if the motorcyclist states they are driving through Canada to Alaska it is a simple matter and they are allowed entry. However, there are no guarantees that a simple answer, or even the proper answer, will permit Canadian entry.

It is not unheard of to have Canadian customs officials completely search a motorcycle. This includes removal of all luggage, disassembling certain parts like headlights, gas tanks and tool compartments. They look for drugs. Be warned.

Motorcyclists can also be asked for proof of ownership of the motorcycle. Canada has computers and a search for stolen vehicles can be done in a matter of minutes. It is advisable to carry a copy of your title as well as your registration.

Proof of insurance can also be requested. Call your insurance carrier before entering Canada to verify coverage. Motorcyclists are advised to carry a Canadian Nonresident Interprovincial Motor Vehicle Liability Insurance card which provides proof of financial responsibility. Available in the U.S. through U.S. insurance carriers or their agents, this card is proof of financial coverage in case of an accident. Financial responsibility has various limits depending on the province of Canada.

One of my traveling friends spent a very long day trying to get into Canada when it was determined he did not have clean paperwork on the motorcycle he had purchased from a dealer in the U.S. just prior to his trip to Alaska. When he became frustrated and surly, his day became worse as the customs officials advised him they could impound his vehicle. He was allowed to return to the U.S. side of the customs station upon the premise that he would have faxed to him at a local fax office a copy of the Bill of Sale from the dealer. However, as it was Monday, the dealer in the U.S. was closed (a fact not known to the border officials). Instead my friend drove 100

Fact Sheet

Entry into Canada for Foreign Nationals with Criminal Convictions or Equivalent

Issue

On June 28, 2002, the implementation of the new *Immigration and Refugee Protection Act* will change the rules affecting the admissibility into Canada of foreign nationals who have criminal convictions in Canada or abroad or who have committed criminal acts outside Canada. These include offences that are considered criminal in Canada, such as driving while under the influence of a substance such as alcohol, even if the offence was not considered a felony or criminal offence in the country where it was committed.

Background Information

- Under Canadian immigration legislation, foreigners who have been convicted of a criminal offence in Canada or abroad or who have committed a criminal act outside Canada may be denied entry into Canada.

- An offence is considered criminal if it is defined in the *Criminal Code of Canada* or other acts of Parliament, regardless of whether the offence is considered criminal in the country where it was committed.

- It is important to note that in Canada, impaired driving is considered a criminal offence, a fact that can take visitors by surprise at the border.

- As of June 28, 2002, under the new *Immigration and Refugee Protection Act*, the following will apply to foreign nationals with criminal convictions.

Deemed Rehabilitation

- A foreign national who has committed one s criminal offence outside Canada may be dee rehabilitated if 10 years have passed since the compl of the sentence imposed and if the person has committed any further criminal acts.

- Deemed rehabilitation applies only to offences tha Canada, would draw a maximum sentence of less 10 years.

- If the foreign national is deemed rehabilitated authorized to enter Canada, there will be administrative fee.

- Immigration Canada officials have the authority to a an individual to enter Canada, based on an assessme risk and other factors at the border examination.

- When an individual has been deemed rehabilitate entry into Canada, this information is not automat entered into government databases. Therefore, vis should not expect to be automatically allowed t enter because they were allowed in on previous v Information on frequent visitors to Canada and o may, however, be entered into the database.

Temporary Resident Permit (TRP)

- At their discretion, Immigration Canada officials allow a foreign national with a criminal convictic enter Canada, even if fewer than 10 years have ela since the imposition of the sentence.

miles to another border crossing where, after he was asked where he lived and where he was going, he was allowed entry.

My best advice to the traveler is have your paperwork in order when crossing into Canada, and be the good Boy Scout by saying "yes sir" and "no sir" when asked to speak. The officials at the border crossings are usually just doing their job. However, like any bureaucrat border officials are empowered to say "no," and they have bad hair days just like anyone else.

Another way you can be prevented from entering Canada by the border officials is if you "lack sufficient funds" to cover the cost of your stay. One of my friends was denied entry for having only $150.00 cash (although he had credit cards). It is an "unwritten rule" that you should have at least $500.00 cash to cover the cost of transit from the border to Alaska.

Waiting for the border crossing to close for the night, such as at the crossing from Haines or Skagway, and then crossing under the closure barrier, is a mistake. Severe fines can be imposed along with confiscation of your vehicle and time in the local jail. This form of entry to Canada is not recommended.

If you have any questions about entering Canada, the best source of information is:

Canadian Government Office of Tourism
"Tourism Canada"
235 Queen St.
Ottawa, ON K1A OH5 Canada

Ask for their travel information brochure.

For telephone inquiries, try Revenue Canada (613) 957-0275.

A Minister's Permit is required for entry into Canada for anyone with a criminal record (including a DWI charge). This requires the filing of paperwork, and in some cases an FBI report, and can take up to six months. While I have not heard of a motorcyclist being stopped at the border for their U.S. DWI, I am sure it has happened. I am aware of a biker stopped

- In this case, the official will issue a Temporary Resident Permit which could be issued at a border point, normally for the duration of the person's visit; however, a longer duration or multiple entries may be granted under certain circumstances.

- There is a $200 Cdn administrative fee required for the issuance of a TRP to cover the cost of processing the application.

- While the TRP can, on occasion, be issued at the border, it is better to apply for this permit ahead of time.

Letter of Rehabilitation

- Some foreign nationals may choose to apply ahead of time to Citizenship and Immigration Canada (CIC) for a Letter of Rehabilitation. The application can be made through Canadian missions abroad. In some circumstances, application can be made at a Canadian border points, although it is advisable to inquire in advance of seeking entry, as a person may be refused entry at the border.

- The Letter of Rehabilitation permanently overcomes the grounds for inadmissibility for a criminal offence, thereby facilitating entry into Canada.

- To cover the costs of processing and background checks on applicants, the fee for this application is either $200 Cdn or $1,000 Cdn, depending on the seriousness of the criminal offence.

- Applicants should note that the fee is non-refundable and that there is no guarantee that an application will be approved, as decisions depend upon the circumstances of each case.

Fast-Track Entry Programs

- Foreign nationals who have committed a criminal offence are automatically disqualified from using pre-clearance systems such as CANPASS or NEXUS.

Contact Information

- For information pertaining to individual cases, travel are advised to contact a Canadian embassy or consu in their country of residence or a Citizenship Immigration office in Canada.

- Contact information for Canadian embassies consulates abroad can be found on the Citizenship Immigration Canada Web site at www.cic.gc.ca or on Department of Foreign Affairs and International Tr Web site at www.dfait.gc.ca

- Automated telephone service is available at Citizens and Immigration Canada Call Centres 7 days/week, hours/day, but calls must be made during the follow hours to speak with an agent:

  (514) 496-1010   Montréal
  8 a.m. – 4 p.m. EST

  (416) 973-4444   Toronto
  8 a.m. – 4 p.m. EST

  (604) 666-2171   Vancouver
  8 a.m. – 4 p.m. PST

  (888) 242-2100   Elsewhere in Canada
  9:30 a.m. – 4 p.m. (local time)

  (888) 576-8502   TTY – text telephone
  8 a.m. – 7 p.m. EST

- Canadian Tourism Commission:

  Lydia McCourt
  Tel: (613) 946-3132
  E-mail: mccourt.lydia@ctc-cct.ca

Disclaimer

The Fact Sheet is intended for your general guidance and convenience of reference only. It is recommended that you consult directly with CIC to ensure that you obtain the latest information and that the advice you receive is based on the fa of a traveller's particular case.

on a speeding charge in Canada who was "deported" without his motorcycle when the computer disclosed he had a criminal record and no Minister's Permit to be in Canada. It could have been worse, he could have been jailed in Canada and fined. I believe the Canadian officials were just saving money by sending him home (he had to pay for his own ticket home, and the speeding ticket). For information regarding Minister's Permits contact:

Canadian Embassy
501 Pennsylvania Ave., N.W.
Washington, D.C. 20001
(202) 682-1740
www.canadianembassy.org

or the nearest Canadian Consulate General.

As mentioned in an earlier chapter, leave the firearms at home. The same with pepper spray. If you are carrying these to "protect yourself from bears," do not worry—if you hit a bear with either you will probably just make it mad. My advice is leave the weapons in a safe place back home and climb a tree if the bear bothers you.

Canada is on the metric system. This means gas is sold in liters or "Imperial Gallons," speed limits and road signs are in kilometers, and temperatures are in Celsius degrees.

For quick reference, below are a couple of tables I use for conversions.

LITERS TO GALLONS

Liters	Gallons	Liters	Gallons
1	.3	6	1.6
2	.5	7	1.8
3	.8	8	2.1
4	1.1	9	2.4
5	1.3	10	2.6

For a quick conversion from kilometers per hour to miles per hour, as you speed past a sign, multiply the kilometers per hour shown on the sign by .6 (actually .62). 90 km/h would equal 55 m/h on an American calibrated speedometer.

Radar is not unknown to law enforcement in Canada. Tickets are as expensive as in the U.S. and often a tourist will be escorted to where they can pay cash. Watch out for Smokey!

LITERS TO GALLONS (continued)

Liters	Gallons	Liters	Gallons
11	2.9	26	6.9
12	3.2	27	7.1
13	3.4	28	7.4
14	3.7	29	7.7
15	4.0	30	7.9
16	4.2	31	8.2
17	4.5	32	8.5
18	4.8	33	8.7
19	5.0	34	9.0
20	5.3	35	9.2
21	5.5	36	9.5
22	5.8	37	9.8
23	6.1	38	10.0
24	6.3	39	10.3
25	6.6	40	10.6

KILOMETERS TO MILES

1	0.6	20	12.4
2	1.2	30	18.6
3	1.9	40	24.8
4	2.5	50	31.1
5	3.1	60	37.3
6	3.7	70	43.5
7	4.3	80	49.7
8	5.0	90	55.9
9	5.6	100	62.1
10	6.2		

All U.S. drivers licenses are valid in Canada. Canada requires motorcycle headlights to be on during the day. Helmets are required. Third party insurance is also required. Check with your insurance company to see if you are covered.

MILES TO KILOMETERS

1	1.6	20	32.2
2	3.2	30	48.3
3	4.8	40	64.4
4	6.4	50	80.5
5	8.0	60	96.5
6	9.6	70	112.6
7	11.3	80	128.7
8	12.9	90	144.8
9	14.5	100	160.9
10	16.1		

SPEEDOMETER SPEEDS (MILES PER HOUR TO KILOMETERS PER HOUR)
Not exact, but neither are most speedometers.

Miles Per Hour		Kilometers Per Hour
20	=	30
30	=	50
40	=	70
55	=	90
60	=	100
70	=	120

TEMPERATURE CONVERSIONS
Fahrenheit to Celsius

Fahrenheit		Celsius
122°	—	50°
120°	—	49°
110°	—	43°
104°	—	40°
100°	—	38°
90°	—	32°
86°	—	30°
80°	—	27°
70°	—	21°
68°	—	20°
60°	—	16°
50°	—	10°
40°	—	4°
32°	—	0°
30°	—	-1°
20°	—	-7°
14°	—	-10°
10°	—	-12°
0°	—	-18°
-4°	—	-20°
-10°	—	-23°
-20°	—	-29°
-22°	—	-30°
-30°	—	-34°
-40°	—	-40°

Canada has some different holidays from the U.S., which can cause some confusion, especially if banking is necessary. Below are listed major Canadian Holidays on which banks and other agencies can be expected to be closed.

MAJOR CANADIAN HOLIDAYS

New Year's Day	Jan. 1
Good Friday	Friday before Easter
Easter Monday	Day after Easter
Victoria Day	May 22
Canada Day	July 1
Alberta Heritage Day	Aug. 1
British Columbia Day	Aug. 1
Discovery Day (YT)	Aug. 21
Labour Day	Sept. 4
Thanksgiving Day	Oct. 9
Remembrance Day	Nov. 11
Christmas Day	Dec. 25
Boxing Day	Dec. 26

CHAPTER 5

THE ROAD TO PRINCE GEORGE, BRITISH COLUMBIA

There are two roads "North to Alaska." Most motorcyclists think only of the Alaska Highway when planning their ride north. This is a mistake, as a perfectly good option is Highway 37 from Kitwanga, British Columbia, to just west of Watson Lake, Yukon Territory. To reach Highway 37 you must travel west from Prince George on the Yellowhead Highway, Highway 16. At Prince George the other option of taking the Alaska Highway from Dawson Creek can be made. From Prince George you can travel north on Highway 97, known as the John Hart Highway or the West Access Route, to Dawson Creek where you connect with the Alaska Highway. Prince George is the decision point.

This section will discuss traveling to Prince George after entering Canada from Washington State. Following sections will describe the Prince George-Kitwanga-Watson Lake route and the Prince George-Dawson Creek Route. For the boating enthusiasts there is a separate chapter on riding the ferryboat.

After crossing the border into Canada, the next destination can be Prince George, British Columbia. Highway 1 from the south leaves the interstate at Hope and heads north as a two-to three-lane highway. Known as the Fraser Canyon Highway, this road runs along the Fraser River, which is a nice canyon ride for over 100 miles. At Cache Creek the road north becomes Highway 97, known as the Cariboo Highway. The road also becomes narrower and passes through long stretches

(**Top**) In the 1800s miners walked to Alaska along the Gold Rush Trail.
(**Bottom**) Downtown 100 Mile House on Highway 97, south of Prince George
between the towns of 93 Mile House and 108 Mile House.

of wooded countryside with farms and ranches. It is over 300 miles from Hope to Prince George. Much of this constitutes the original Gold Rush Trail taken by fortune hunters as they hiked north to the gold fields of Alaska and Yukon Territory.

Prince George is the last major city (population 71,000) you will pass through until you reach Fairbanks or Anchorage. It is a modern city with several large hotels, three major motorcycle shops (Harley Davidson, Honda, Yamaha and Suzuki), many motels and a full-service private campground.

If you are going to need a tire, Prince George is not where you should plan on getting it. I once stopped in a motorcycle shop and they had four (4) tires in their tire inventory, and those four were very expensive. When I asked the owner about their low inventory, he explained that it was not unusual for that time of the year (August). It seems he would order what he planned for use by his local customers to be used by late summer. As there is almost no motorcycling in the fall and winter, any leftover inventory would remain on the shelf until spring, thereby tying up his working capital which he needed for winter sport vehicles like snowmobiles and ATVs. He said that if one of his local customers needed a tire and he was out of stock he would order it shipped in, which would only take a day or two. That is fine for the local customers, but hard on the tourist traveling through on their way to Alaska and on a schedule. My advice for tires is have fresh ones when you cross the border into Canada and do not plan on making a change until you reach Anchorage or Fairbanks.

Prince George is a good stopping point for the night as it has stores which can supply you with those last-minute items you remembered you forgot to purchase before you left the U.S. From here north, or west, mercantile facilities become less well-stocked. Prince George also has a number of restaurants and even several fast food places.

At Prince George you can either continue north to Dawson Creek or turn west to take the Cassiar Highway to Watson Lake.

CHAPTER 6

PRINCE GEORGE TO DAWSON CREEK — MILEPOST -0- — ON THE ALASKA HIGHWAY

It is 250 miles from Prince George to Dawson Creek. North from Prince George, follow Highway 97, the John Hart Highway, the entire distance. Highway 97 is a two-lane, paved highway with both straight and winding sections. It was named after John Hart, former British Columbia premier, who sponsored its construction. Driving time is approximately four hours.

Throughout your travels north you will find road construction. Some of this is due to weather damage to the roads and some is due to general maintenance. Some construction projects have no explanation. Often the traffic will be halted. Mosquitoes like these stops because it gives them a chance to enjoy fresh food from tourists who get out of their cars or leave windows rolled down. Motorcyclists are advised to keep their helmets on or apply mosquito repellent. The construction workers often wear mosquito-net headgear.

PRINCE GEORGE NORTH ON
JOHN HART HIGHWAY (97)

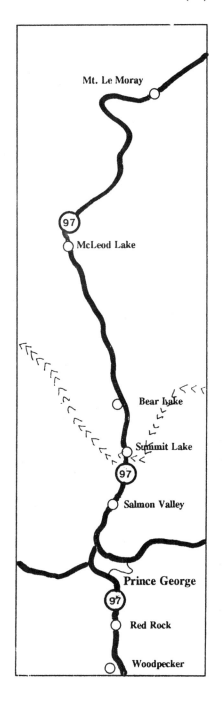

(**Top**) Another way to arrive in Dawson Creek is from Alberta via Highway 2 and Edmonton. (**Bottom**) Mount Robson Park, west of Jasper, is a picturesque ride.

HIGHWAY 97 INTO DAWSON CREEK
AND HUDSON'S HOPE LOOP

Sixty-two miles west of Dawson Creek is the town of Chetwynd on Highway 97. Here you can turn north and avoid Dawson Creek by taking Highway 29. This 87-mile road is a shortcut to the Alaska Highway. It was first built in the 1950s from the Alaska Highway to the W.A.C. Bennett Dam on the Peace River. In 1968, the highway was pushed through to Chetwynd. It is a nice, winding road that runs along the Peace River from Hudson's Hope to just northwest of Fort St. John. If you want to save a few miles and ride an interesting road, Hudson's Hope Loop is a fun ride.

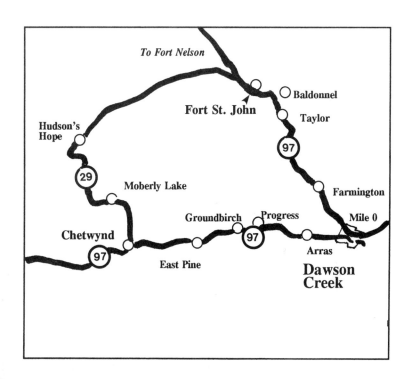

CHAPTER 7

DAWSON CREEK TO ALASKA —
THE ALASKA HIGHWAY

The Alaska Highway is 1,520 miles in length and stretches from Dawson Creek to Fairbanks. There are several good publications describing the entire length of the Alaska Highway. The most popular is THE MILE POST. This 750-page publication is updated annually and lists everything from motels, campgrounds, restaurants, roadhouses, to even turnoffs and visitor information signs along the entire length of the Alaska Highway. About the only thing it does not list is where a bear will run across the road in front of you, but it does describe where along the routes you should watch out for bears. This publication costs $24.95 and is available from:

Morris Communications Corp.
P.O. Box 1668
Augusta, GA 30903
www.themilepost.com

or by calling 1-800-726-4707.

There are two "Beginning of the Alaska Highway" signs in Dawson Creek. The original sign (above), or Milepost 0, is located downtown Dawson Creek, about four blocks from the newer sign at the Tourist Information Bureau near the traffic circle. As the Alaska Highway became popular, more and more automobiles stopped in the main street downtown, in traffic, to take pictures of the original marker, causing traffic havoc. The city fathers decided to erect another sign, with parking, off the main street so tourists could park and take pictures. Thus, the sign at the Tourist Information Bureau. Motorcycles parking in front of the downtown sign seem not to get much attention, so if you want a picture of the original, look for the one downtown.

Once you start up the Alaska Highway you can expect weather ranging from hot and dusty to snow and rain, in the months of July and August. An all-weather riding suit like those offered by Aerostitch can save the rider time and inconvenience. Here a rider demonstrates rain gloves from Aerostitch that I call the "Spock-gloves." They easily slip on and off over my riding gloves and fold up into a compact ball I keep in the side pockets of my tank bag.

The "forest" in the background is what you will see miles and miles of as you move further north. More like scrub brush than Lower 48 pine trees, the fir trees offer little protection in rain, or from bears if you try to climb one.

Several of the bridges along the Alaska Highway use these metal grates for road surface. A narrow tire on the motorcycle crossing this grating will cause the motorcycle to "weave." They are especially dangerous when wet. Exercise extreme caution when driving onto this type of bridge. Slow down when you approach one.

DAWSON CREEK TO FT. NELSON

Map Explanation:

My maps show mileage from Dawson Creek, in kilometers. A box with GF and mileage means "Gas," "Food," and how many kilometers from Dawson Creek. "GFL" means "GAS" "FOOD" and "Lodging" with mileage.

G = Gas
L = Lodging
F = Food

Approaching Taylor, 35 miles (55 kilometers) out of Dawson Creek, you will cross a cantilever and truss bridge over 2,000 feet long, with metal grating which causes numerous motorcycle crashes. Local motorcyclists drive on the concrete sidewalk. Be careful if you will need to cross on the metal grating, especially if it is wet.

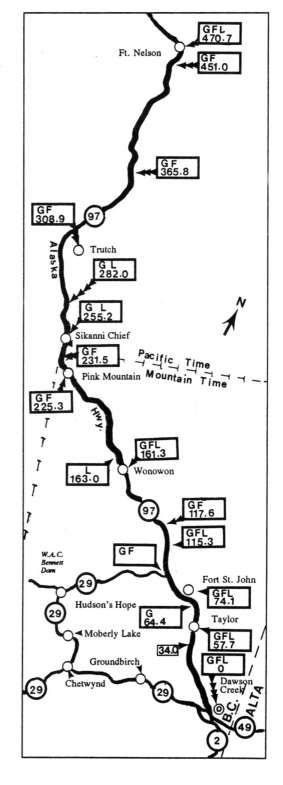

(Top) Signs give warning of rough road ahead. It is easy to forget the warning after several miles, as the road smooths out, but it will get rough again and turn to gravel. Remember how long the warnings are for. **(Bottom)** Mistakes are made by automobiles, trucks and motorcycles. There are many stories about motorcycle crashes along the Alaska Highway, usually caused by gravel or construction.

(**Top**) Construction is an ongoing project along the Alaska Highway. Sometimes the road construction can go on for miles. Soft gravel or mud often causes motorcycles to go down. (**Bottom**) Radiator protector served well to catch rocks, mud and bugs. Motorcyclists should find a plastic covering for their headlights, as small stones break many.

75

Kilometer posts are located on the right-hand side of the Alaska Highway every 3 miles (5 kilometers). They are white numbers on green signs. After you enter Yukon Territory just east of Watson Lake, the kilometer posts are white posts with black numbers every 1.2 miles (2 kilometers).

FT. NELSON TO WATSON LAKE

Two passes, Summit Lake Pass and Muncho Pass, can experience snow in the summer. The road is rough and narrow. Watch for animals, especially Stone Sheep and Caribou. Tourists make sudden and unpredictable stops along this section to take photos. Muncho Lake is one of the most scenic spots on the Alaska Highway. Liard River Hot Springs Park has a free hot springs and public campground ($15.00 and up). Watson Lake is home of the "Signpost Forest." People place signs on the high fence from all over the world. Watson Lake is known as "The Gateway to The Yukon." You are now in Yukon Territory.

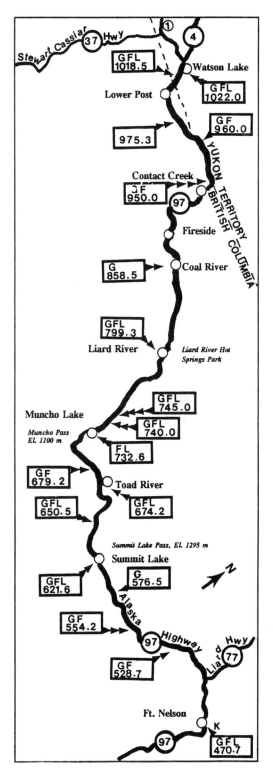

Stewart Cassiar 37 Hwy

1

4

GFL 1018.5

Watson Lake

Lower Post

GFL 1022.0

GF 960.0

975.3

YUKON TERRITORY

BRITISH COLUMBIA

Contact Creek

GF 950.0

97

Fireside

G 858.5

Coal River

GFL 799.3

Liard River

Liard River Hot Springs Park

GFL 745.0

GFL 740.0

Muncho Lake

Muncho Pass EL 1100 m

FL 732.6

GF 679.2

Toad River

GFL 650.5

GFL 674.2

Summit Lake Pass, El. 1295 m

Summit Lake

GFL 621.6

G 576.5

N

GF 554.2

97 Highway

Liard Hwy

77

GF 528.7

Alaska

Ft. Nelson

K

97

GFL 470.7

(**Top and bottom**) Upper pool at Liard River Hot Springs. The lower pool has a changing room and many more people.

Liard River Hot Springs. From the parking lot to the hot springs is about one-quarter mile. This boardwalk runs the entire distance. In the early 1970s, we would flog our motorcycles through these woods to camp out next to the hot springs. That is now prohibited. The parties at the hot springs have also been prohibited, but some of the locals can still tell wild stories about what went on in the '60s and '70s.

TESLIN

THE COMMUNITY OF TESLIN WAS ORIGINALLY A SUMMER
HOME OF TLINGIT INDIANS FROM COASTAL ALASKA AND
BRITISH COLUMBIA. DURING THE KLONDIKE GOLD RUSH.
THE SETTLEMENT BOOMED BRIEFLY AS A STOP ON
THE "ALL-CANADIAN ROUTE" TO DAWSON. VIA THE
HOOTALINQUA (NOW TESLIN) RIVER. THE PRESENT TOWNSITE
WAS ESTABLISHED AS A PERMANENT TRADING POST BY
1905. AND WAS SERVICED BY STERNWHEELERS FROM
WHITEHORSE UNTIL THE ALASKA HIGHWAY WAS BUILT
IN 1942.

From Watson Lake to Teslin, approximately 160 miles, the countryside is mostly unpopulated except for a few gas stations and lodges. This is a mountainous section of Yukon Territory with the Cassiar Mountains to the left and the Pelly Mountains to the right. You will be leaving the Rocky Mountains as you enter Teslin. The next mountains you encounter to the west are part of the Cascade Range extending down into Washington and Oregon. Teslin has a population of approximately 350.

WATSON LAKE TO WHITEHORSE

Approximately 140 kilometers west of Watson Lake, you will cross the Continental Divide. After this point, all rivers crossed to Fairbanks drain into the Yukon River. As you approach Teslin, beware of the bridge! Whitehorse is the largest city in Yukon Territory. With a population of 22,526, it supports several motorcycle shops. Prices are very high. There are several campgrounds in and around Whitehorse. The public one in town requires that you park your motorcycle in a common parking lot and carry your gear to your camp. Takhini Hot Springs, northwest of town, is owned by a local Indian tribe. There are no showers in their campground, but a shower is free when you pay to go into the hot springs pool. Firewood is free.

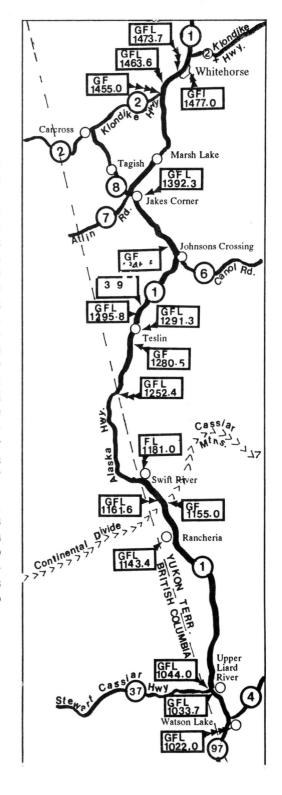

(Top) Bridge warning east of Teslin. **(Bottom)** Nisutlin Bay Bridge at Teslin. There are no sidewalks on which to ride. This is the site of numerous motorcycle crashes each summer.

(**Top**) A bad day for Mr. Yukon Gopher. He got his paw caught in a gopher trap. (**Bottom**) Mr. Yukon Gopher's day gets worse when village dogs find him.

(**Top**) West of Whitehorse a section of the old Alaska Highway. The turnoff is well-marked. Highway is to the south of the main Alaska Highway. (**Bottom**) New Alaska Highway west of Whitehorse into Haines Junction.

WHITEHORSE TO TOK, ALASKA

As you pass through Champagne, an Indian Village west of Whitehorse, do not stop and take pictures of the Indian cemetery. It is not a tourist attraction. Approximately 100 miles west of Whitehorse is Haines Junction. Here the Alaska Highway meets the Haines Highway (Yukon Highway 3). In Haines Junction, make a right turn; otherwise, you will drive to Haines, a nice ride, but not going to the part of Alaska that is to the northwest. The ferryboat from Bellingham, Washington, arrives in Haines. Watch for buffalo west of Haines; the local Indian tribe has a large herd. The road from Burwash Landing to Beaver Creek is part of the original Alaska Highway and very rough. Trailers scrape the road surface and sometimes become detached. The swells are caused by frost heaves, which any new road would also have unless built above ground. The international border sign for pictures is past Canadian customs and before the U.S. border station.

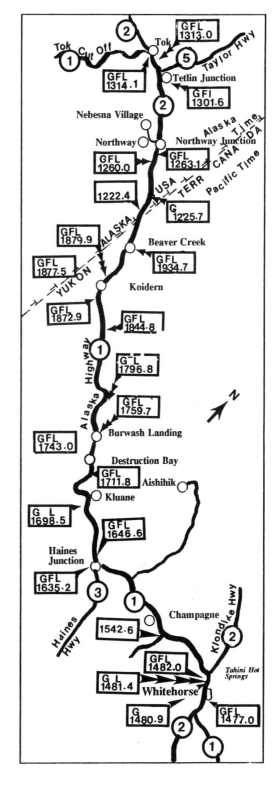

(Top) In downtown Haines Junction (population less than 1,000) make the right turn toward Fairbanks. **(Bottom)** Kluane Lake is glacial fed and sometimes nearly turquoise in color.

(Top) While Canada is on the metric system, some businesses cater to American traffic. Here, a series of signs in Canada give directions in miles. **(Bottom)** Not all motorcycles are driven the whole length of the Highway. Some break.

87

(Top) Do not expect five star restaurants along the Alaska Highway. **(Bottom)** A rare sign offering a breakfast special from days past. Gas can be $8.00 per gallon.

Some samples of motorcycles and drivers who drove to Alaska.

(Top) Two up from California. **(Bottom)** Solo from Connecticut.

90

Two Goldwings, top from Colorado, bottom from California. Lower driver was
71 years young.

(Top) Lady driver from Wisconsin. **(Bottom)** Kawasaki and driver from Kansas at Alaska border on Alaska Highway.

Motorcyclists entering Alaska at Alaska Highway border crossing 1,189 miles from Dawson Creek. Time zones change here from Pacific Time in Yukon Territory to Alaska Time in Alaska. Named Port Alcan, this border crossing is open 24 hours a day.

94

CHAPTER 8

PRINCE GEORGE TO ALASKA HIGHWAY
VIA STEWART-CASSIAR HIGHWAY

This is the alternate route to Alaska. Instead of going north and east from Prince George to Dawson Creek to connect with

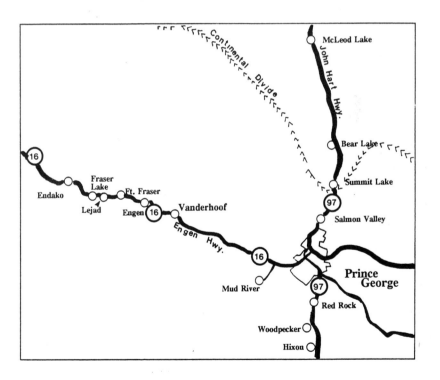

This building was originally owned by Barney Mulvaney, packer, trapper, adventurer, who set up a tent town in 1914 in what became Burns Lake. In 1917 he had the townsite surveyed and sold lots. This cabin which was located next to his hotel "The Cheslatta" and later known as "The Omineca", became a gambling hall nicknamed...

"The Bucket of Blood."

(Top) Visitor Center at Fraser Lake. Good for free maps and information on the area. **(Bottom)** Burns Lake, population 2,300, has four gas stations, a visitor center on the west end of town, and offers "3,000 miles of fishing."

the start of the Alaska Highway, you can drive west and north to connect with the Alaska Highway just west of Watson Lake. This is known as the most direct route to Alaska and is often avoided by motorcyclists because they see the major highway north, the Stewart-Cassiar Highway, as a gravel road on most current maps. Each year more of this highway is paved and at the time of this writing less than 100 miles remains gravel. It is also one of the more picturesque highways in British Columbia. The gravel sections remaining are generally high-speed sections and any type of motorcycle, piloted by a reasonably competent driver, can negotiate the gravel sections. The facilities along the route north are not five star, but gas, food, and lodging are available. There is often construction on the Stewart-Cassiar Highway, so expect delays.

The first section of road is from Prince George, west on Highway 16 to the junction of Highway 37, 306 miles in distance. This junction has a gas station and café, where you should fill your gas tank for the road north, as gas is sparse after this.

(Top) 'KSAN Campground next to Skeena River, New Hazelton, B.C. Heavy fog. **(Bottom)** Campground life. Before starting up Cassiar Highway, a motorcyclist mounts the new rear tire he has been carrying since Seattle.

98

Smithers is 250 miles from Prince George and is a major ski area for British Columbia. Its Swiss-style storefronts and Hudson Bay Mountain in the background remind you of Switzerland. Twenty miles west of Smithers is Moricetown Canyon on the Bulkley River, in July an Indian net fishing site. Nearby Moricetown is an Indian village and surrounding reservation.

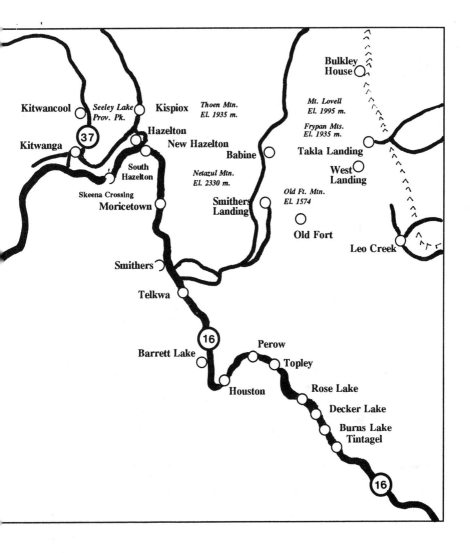

(Top) Gitwangak totem poles, Kitwanga, just off Highway 37 north. **(Bottom)** 'KSAN Indian Village long house.

100

The last major town before turning north on Highway 37 is New Hazelton (population in the area is 1,300). Here there are motels, gas stations and restaurants. The old town, Hazelton, is historically interesting. A nice campground with showers is located next to the 'KSAN Indian Village, a replica Gitsan Indian village. This area is rich in Indian culture and known for totem poles ("Totem Pole capital of the World"). This is a good area to spend a day "touristing," doing laundry and generally taking it easy before starting up the Cassiar Highway. If you need any work done to your motorcycle, such as a tire change (if you have your own tire), oil change or welding, this is where you should get it done.

A day-ride down Highway 16 to Prince Rupert (population is the area around 21,000), about 150 miles each direction, can easily round out a day of "R & R" in the area.

As for touristing, the Hagwilget Canyon, as you cross the Bulkley River between New Hazelton and Hazelton, is one of the most photographed places in Canada.

If you arrive during the annual salmon run you can watch the Native fishermen netting giant salmon (if they are lucky) in the rapids. This is done by using dip-nets attached to 20-40 foot-long pine poles. This is an extremely dangerous form of fishing and you will see the Natives with ropes tied around their middles in case they are pulled off the rock precipices by the fast-moving water or a 40-50 lb. salmon. The combined weight of the pole, net and fish can often weigh as much as 100 lbs.

(Top) Paved road along Kitsumkalum Lake. **(Bottom)** Road turns to gravel. Watch out for logging trucks.

HAZELTON TO TERRACE TO STEWART-CASSIAR HIGHWAY

For the more adventuresome motorcyclist, an interesting side trip is through the Nass Valley/Kalum Lake to Cranberry Junction, where you can connect with Highway 37 forty-eight miles north of the junction with Highway 16.

Instead of turning north at Highway 37, proceed west on Highway 16 to Terrace, about 60 miles farther west. There, turn north at the sign to Kalum Lake/Nass Valley on the Nisga'a Highway. This Nisga'a Highway is paved for nearly 20 miles. Shown on many maps as a logging road which was closed to traffic during the week, it is now open to Cranberry Junction and Greenville. There are no facilities on this road, and also very little traffic other than logging trucks and an occasional tourist. I once met a German motorcyclist out here who I thought was lost, but he was "exploring" he said, "looking for what lies at the end of the road." I traveled with him for a week and we found several ends of roads. This side trip on the Nisga'a Highway is seldom traveled, but well worth taking the time to see some of the more remote areas of British Columbia.

(**Top**) Gravel road along lake, seldom traveled, especially during the week.
(**Bottom**) Junction. West to Greenville, east to Cranberry Junction (Highway
37).

(Top) Logging road, not recommended during wet weather. (Bottom) Back country advertisement for "Mushroom Buyer."

(**Top**) Gas station/cafe at junction of Highway 16 and Highway 37. Get gas here. If closed, go back to New Hazelton for gas. (**Bottom**) Watch for these signs. If you cannot make 141 kilometers on your remaining gas, turn around and fill up.

STEWART-CASSIAR HIGHWAY

Cassiar Highway (37) from the junction of Highway 16 to Alaska Highway is 456 miles. Two side trips can be taken, one to Stewart-Hyder (Alaska), and one to Telegraph Creek. Sections of the Cassiar Highway are unpaved. The Highway Department uses a calcium mix on the gravel sections, which turns hard with water. It also hardens on motorcycles and clothing. Wash your motorcycle/leathers upon leaving gravel sections of the Cassiar Highway. I still have some of the calcium on my motorcycle from four years ago, which I failed to wash off soon enough. Get gasoline when you see it. Gas stations close early or go out of business from year to year. If the gas station at Meziadin Junction is closed, go left toward Hyder about a mile and try the boat dock gas station. The Cassiar area is a very remote section of British Columbia. As more of the road is paved, traffic will increase. Because of the current gravel sections there are many crashes — I call this a "Crash and Burn Highway," for the numerous crashes . . . many of them at high speed.

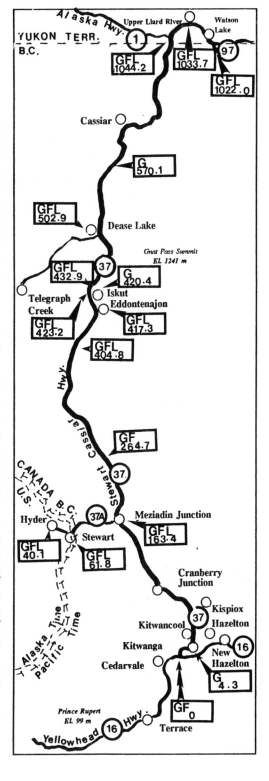

A wooden bridge still in use on the Cassiar Highway. These are fine when the road surface is dry, but very slick when wet. On these narrow bridges yield to oncoming trucks, as they will not yield to you. The Cassiar Highway was originally a logging road. In the early '70s and late '60s, it was mud ruts and very slow travel for motorcyclists. It is along one of the original routes considered for the ALCAN Highway from Alaska to the United States. I am sorry to see that it is being paved, as it is one of the more remote areas you can pass through on your way to Alaska. This will change with more traffic. It is a very long day-ride from New Hazelton to Watson Lake, especially if a side trip is taken.

SIDE TRIP: STEWART, B.C., HYDER, ALASKA

At Meziadin Junction, you can turn west to Stewart, B.C., 41 miles away. A paved road twists down the valley of the Stromm Creek past a picturesque glacier, Bear Glacier (watch for bears). 2.5 miles past Stewart (population 1,000) is the town of Hyder, Alaska (population 85). If you are in a hurry to reach Alaska, you can go to Hyder and beat others trying to make Alaska by three days. Hyder, known for its nightlife, has earned a reputation and town motto as "The Friendliest Little Ghost Town in Alaska." Hyder is also known for a very strong alcohol drink which you can get at one of the local bars, after which you can say you have been "Hyderized."

There is gas in Stewart and several restaurants/cafes. Round trip from Meziadin Junction is approximately two hours, if you do not get Hyderized.

(**Top**) Trucks on Cassiar Highway do not slow down for motorcycles or cars. Beware of flying stones and dust. (**Bottom**) Get gas when you see it. It will be expensive. Do not expect to use your gold charge card. Cash may be all they accept.

110

There are no "mileposts" or "kilometreposts" along the Cassiar Highway as there are along the Alaska Highway. Keep an eye on your speedometer for mileage to advise you how far the next gas stop is. This road is well-traveled during the summer months, with nearly everything from motorhomes to motorcycles with sidecars and trailers traveling up it.

111

Typical of gas stations, accommodations, and repair shops along the Cassiar Highway is this one at the Tatogga Lake Resort.

A rest stop along the Cassiar Highway. Notice the calcium deposits on the riders' leathers.

Buildings from Telegraph Creek, British Columbia. Telegraph Creek does not see many motorcyclists during the year. I like the town because it is so remote and away from the general tourist traffic of the Cassiar Highway, of which there is not much. Do not tell your motorhome friends about Telegraph Creek, or there will soon be a paved road out there also.

114

SIDE TRIP: DEASE LAKE TO TELEGRAPH CREEK

This side trip is not recommended for the timid traveler. All 75 miles of the road to Telegraph Creek are gravel, with some steep, narrow sections and several sets of switchbacks. RVs and cars pulling trailers are not recommended for travel to Telegraph Creek, so these "road beasts" are absent.

Telegraph Creek was a major jumping off point for gold miners to the Yukon. They would ride the ferryboat from Seattle to Telegraph Creek and then walk the rest of the way to the Alaska goldfields, or at least to Whitehorse. It now has a population of about 300. There is gas, a lodge and cafe. Because of the road conditions, allow about an hour and one-half to drive to Telegraph Creek.

Jade is prevalent in the area. Chinese graves of jade seekers have been found in caves above the road, from a period of time long before Columbus landed on the eastern shores of North America.

Moose Meadows Camping on Cotton Lake, 53 miles north of Dease Lake. Camping, no electric, no telephones, but beautiful scenery and the cry of Loons. Hot showers and some covered tenting sites.

(Top) Camping at Moose Meadows for the more rugged traveler. It is not a KOA. **(Bottom)** Former trapper, outdoorsman and Hollywood entertainer Mighty Moe used to own the place and stories of his years in the area make for tall tales.

117

Not all small planes in Alaska and Canada land on water. Do not be surprised to see one land in front of or behind you. In some places the highway is used as a landing strip.

Just west of Watson Lake, the Cassiar Highway runs into the Alaska Highway. From here, proceed west to Alaska. There is a gas station, motel and restaurant at this junction.

CHAPTER 9

ANOTHER ROAD TO ALASKA: TOP-OF-THE-WORLD HIGHWAY

Instead of following the Alaska Highway to the ALCAN Border Station, there is an alternate route to Alaska which takes you through Dawson City and over the Top-Of-The-World Highway and across the highest U.S. border crossing in North America.

At Watson Lake, you have three options to Dawson City:

(1)   The Campbell Highway to Carmacks, then north to Dawson City.

(2)   The Canol Road to Ross River, then west on the Campbell Highway to Carmacks, then north to Dawson City.

(3)   The Alaska Highway to Whitehorse, then north to Dawson City on Highway 2.

The first two of these choices will find you traveling over long stretches of gravel road through unpopulated areas, until you reach Carmacks. The third choice is a paved road to Dawson. If you take option number 1, you avoid nearly all of the Alaska Highway and leave it for your return trip. Many travelers take the ferryboat to Alaska because they say they do not want to travel the Alaska Highway both directions. By taking the Cassiar-Campbell and Top-Of-The-World Highway

From Watson Lake to Ross River, there are no gas stations, or anything else, for 232 miles. The road is gravel and in reasonably good condition when dry. When wet, it is very slippery in places and slow going for the motorcyclist. There are several public campgrounds along the road and some of the biggest clouds of mosquitoes I have encountered in the north. It was hard not to inhale them through my nose when stopped. There is also a lot of wildlife along this route, especially in the evening. I was nearly run over by a black bear one night as he charged out of the woods, seemingly oblivious to me and my motorcycle, as I rode along at 60 miles per hour.

route, only 14 miles of the Alaska Highway are ridden twice, between Tok, Alaska, and Dawson Creek.

Campbell Highway

The Campbell Highway is 373 miles of mostly gravel road through very primitive areas. Between Watson Lake and Ross River, there is no gas (there is one gas station which has been occasionally open, but I usually find it closed). It is 232 miles of wilderness. At Ross River, there is a store, gas station, and restaurants. From Ross River, it is 140 miles to Carmacks, where you turn north on Highway 2 to Dawson City. The one town in between, Faro (population 500), is a modern mining town with full services. The ride from Watson Lake to Carmacks takes approximately 6 hours and often you can travel the entire distance between Watson Lake and Ross River without passing another vehicle.

Canol Road

West of Teslin on the Alaska Highway, the Canol Road (Highway 6) starts north just before Johnson's Crossing. It is a winding, twisty gravel road for 136 miles to Ross River. From Ross River, you can take the Campbell Highway to Carmacks (see above). There are no services on the Canol Road, and seldom other travelers.

Highway 2

This paved highway from Whitehorse, known as the Klondike Loop to Alaska, is 327 miles to Dawson City. It is a well-traveled road with plenty of gas, food and lodging stops along the way. Dawson City has legal gambling, so there is

(Top) Ross River ferryboat crossing of the Pelly River to Canol Road north.
(Bottom) Touring motorcycles may want to stop their trip north here.

quite a flow of traffic from Whitehorse and back, especially on the weekends.

All three of the above routes end in Dawson at the Yukon River. From here, the motorcyclist can take a small ferryboat (free) across the Yukon River, and then ride the Top-Of-The-World Highway to the Alaska-Canada border station 66 miles away. The border stations are open from 9:00 a.m. - 9:00 p.m. (Pacific Time) during the summer months on the Canadian side and 8:00 a.m. to 8:00 p.m. on the U.S. side (Alaska time). From here it is 12 miles to Jack Wade Junction, where you connect with the Taylor Highway and start south to the Alaska Highway 95 miles away. Some of this route is unpaved. While this is a well-traveled road, and unpaved for a major portion, it often sees motorhomes, tour buses and trailers wallowing over it. Be prepared to ride over some very slippery sections if wet or under construction. The unpaved sections are not kind to overburdened touring motorcycles with nearly smooth highway tires.

(**Top**) If the ferryboat at Ross River is closed, it means it is not running. (**Bottom**) A determined motorcyclist can take the motorcycle apart and borrow a canoe to get across a river.

126

SIDE TRIP: ROSS RIVER TO NORTHWEST TERRITORIES

The north Canol Road is 144 miles to the border of Northwest Territories. It is unpaved and unserviced. This side trip is recommended for only the experienced adventurer. While the scenery is worth the trip, a mistake can be costly. I once cracked my crankcase on this road near its end. While I was able to repair the crack, I had lost all my oil and had nothing with which to refill the crankcase. After three days of eating berries and some unlucky squirrels and small birds, I was "discovered" by a hunter who had enough supplies to get me back to Ross River.

There is a trail from the end of the Canol Road to Norman Wells, a distance of about 230 miles. It has been designated a Heritage Trail and some people hike it. From Ross River to Norman Wells, you would have to have enough gas to go 375 miles, some of it through deep streams and over washouts.

PUBLIC DRINKING
PROHIBITED
WITHIN 5 km
OF PELLY CROSSING
COMMUNITY CENTRE
By Order in Council

(**Top**) The Five Fingers, site of many ferryboat crashes during the gold
rush. On the Yukon River, between Carmacks and Dawson City. (**Bottom**)
Pelly Crossing, Silkirk Indian Community, below Dawson City.

128

Dawson City as seen from the Yukon River. A population of nearly 2,200 is supported by tourist business and gambling. There is still some gold mining in the area. Dawson City is a good stopping place for the night, as there are campgrounds, motels, restaurants and gas stations. The main street still has wooden sidewalks and many of the buildings from the gold rush days still serve as businesses. The motorcyclists passing through Dawson City to and from Alaska tend to have a more hardened look and the motorcycles appear well worn.

The ferryboat from Dawson City across the Yukon River is free and takes about 15 minutes, but in the high season you may have to wait 2-3 hours due to backed-up traffic. There is no dock on either side of the river, so the ferryboat driver "plows" into the bank and then drops the loading ramp. I recommend the motorcyclist be ready to steady the motorcycle when the ferryboat comes into shore, as it can rock off the center stand or side stand with the sudden stop.

(**Top**) International boundary, Poker Creek, Alaska. (**Bottom**) Poker Creek, Top-Of-The-World Highway, population 2.

131

(Top) Welcome to Alaska, Top-Of-The-World Highway. **(Bottom)** Boundry is a town, not the border. Gas available.

(**Top**) Downtown Chicken, Alaska, population 40, in the "high season."
(**Bottom**) Gas at Chicken is expensive, but so is everything else in Alaska. Last
gas until Tok, on the Alaska Highway.

CHAPTER 10

THE ALASKA MARINE HIGHWAY —
THE FERRYBOAT NORTH

Riding a motorcycle to Alaska can take another form of travel, the ferryboat. A three-night trip from Bellingham, Washington, to Haines, Alaska, takes the motorcyclist up the famed "Inland Passage." In the summer, the ferryboat usually departs from Bellingham (85 miles north of Seattle) in the early evening (6:00 p.m.). The Alaska Ferry does not stop in Canada en route to Alaska. The first stop will be in Ketchikan, Alaska, thirty-six hours after leaving Bellingham.

The ferryboat is not inexpensive. A motorcycle will cost nearly $400, plus $300 per person, between Bellingham and Haines. A bunk in a cabin can cost between $230 and $400 more, depending on whether the cabin has a window (facing outside) and how many bunks are in the cabin. A trailer on the back of a motorcycle will cost as much as the motorcycle.

Upon arrival in Haines, Alaska, the motorcyclist must drive 152 miles north on the Haines Highway to Haines Junction where they can connect with the Alaska Highway. They will enter Canada 41 miles outside of Haines and must go through the same customs requirements as if they had crossed into Canada at any other border crossing.

Some motorcyclists ride the ferryboat to Skagway and drive from there to east of Whitehorse, where they connect with the Alaska Highway or continue north to Dawson City. At Whitehorse, they continue on the Alaska Highway to Alaska or

(**Top**) Alaska Ferry departs from Bellingham, Washington. (**Bottom**) Terminal, Alaska Ferry, Bellingham, Washington. Plan to arrive early.

go north to Dawson City, then to Alaska via the Top-Of-The-World Highway.

Reservations are an absolute must for all motorcyclists on the Alaska Ferry in the summer months.

For information on the Alaska Ferry:

Alaska Marine Highway
6858 Glacier Highway
Juneau, Alaska 99801-7909
Telephone: (800) 642-0066
www.alaska.gov/ferry

In Alaska you can find bumper stickers that read, "I Rode My Motorcycle To Alaska!" It is estimated that nearly 50% of all motorcycles reaching Alaska in the summer have done so by the ferry system.

There are some pluses and minuses to riding the ferry to Alaska. On the plus side is less wear on pilot, chains and tires, so that once you reach Alaska your motorcycle is "fresh" versus wearing out parts on the long ride up. Additional pluses are the relaxing pace through the Inland Passage. On the minus side are the high costs and the weather, which often is foggy or raining the entire trip.

In terms of time, the ride up through British Columbia to Haines Junction and the time spent in the ferry system is about the same and the scenery outstanding either way. With gas, food and sleeping on the road route you will spend about as much as you would for the boat trip.

Each summer an increasing number of motorcycles are being crated and sent from Seattle to Anchorage (and return), either by boat or air. For the time-pressed rider this is an option that can save nearly two weeks each way, leaving more time to explore Alaska and the Northwest Territories of Canada.

(**Top**) Alaska Ferry at Bellingham, Washington. (**Bottom**) Entrance to the ferryboat.

(**Top**) Cabin view of the Inland Passage from cabin with a window. (Photo by Jim Sanders) (**Bottom**) "Deck passage" is the cheapest fare to Alaska. (Photo by Jim Sanders)

(**Top**) Motorcycles waiting in line to board ferryboat to Alaska. (Photo by Jim Sanders) (**Bottom**) Motorcycles tied down inside ferryboat. Access is limited while in transit. (Photo by Jim Sanders)

Some views of the sights along the Inside Passage to Alaska. (Photos by Jim Sanders)

Downtown Haines, Alaska. Next to the last stop on the Alaska Marine Highway. 152 miles away is the Alaska Highway. Several years ago, we had some fun with a couple of "bikers" who trailered their motorcycles to Bellingham, then rode the ferryboat to Alaska. We knew they would stop at all the Harley Davidson shops in Alaska to purchase a souvenir tee shirt for their collections. We contacted each shop and let them know these fellows would be arriving and what day they were expected. Upon their arrival in the motorcycle shop they were greeted with, "Oh, you're the fellows who rode up here ON THE FERRYBOAT!" Their chagrin was enough for them not to talk about the ferryboat ride or show pictures when they got home. We have done the same with other brand motorcycle riders, but most of them at least rode their motorcycles to Bellingham.

HAINES, ALASKA, TO HAINES JUNCTION, YUKON TERRITORY; SKAGWAY TO WHITEHORSE, YUKON TERRITORY

Haines to Haines Junction, and the Alaska Highway, is 152 miles.

Skagway to Alaska Highway is 99 miles.

Both routes leave Alaska and enter British Columbia, then Yukon Territory.

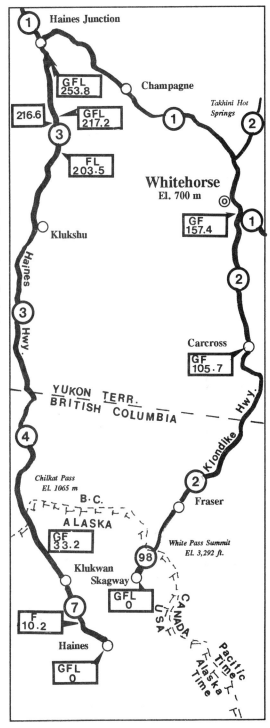

George Rahn

CHAPTER 11

TO FAIRBANKS

You have reached Alaska!! From the ALCAN Border Station to Fairbanks is nearly 300 miles. For the first 100 miles, watch for potholes, frost heaves and pavement breaks. Tok, Alaska, has several gas stations/ restaurants/motels and campgrounds. Also a well-known bakery. Tok to Delta Junction is approximately 100 miles. Delta Junction is the official end of the ALASKA HIGHWAY. From here to Fairbanks, the highway is known as the Richardson Highway.

Delta Junction to Fairbanks is approximately 100 miles. Fairbanks, population 83,000, has several motorcycle shops. One, Trail's End-BMW, is famous for its owner George Rahn, who rode a BMW motorcycle to Alaska in the early 1960s and never left. Either the Alaska Highway was so tough on George he did not want to ride back, or he loved Alaska so much he decided to stay. (If you meet George, you will learn he rides all year, so it must have been the love of Alaska that caused him to stay.)

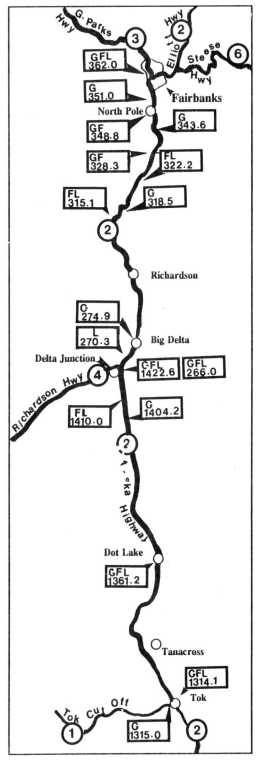

This sign is at the end of the Alaska Highway, Delta Junction, Mile 1422.

146

CHAPTER 12

TO ANCHORAGE

From Tok, Alaska, to Anchorage is 328 miles. The entire road is paved, although often sections are under repair.

Anchorage, Alaska, population approximately 250,000, is Alaska's largest city. Several motorcycle dealers are supported by an active motorcycle owners group in the area. Try to schedule service and tire changes well in advance (two weeks) in the summer months.

Anchorage has all those conveniences you may have missed since leaving the Lower 48 . . . K-mart, McDonalds, Jiffy Lube and quick-stop gas stations. It also has rush hour traffic and parking meters.

The public campground in Anchorage takes reservations and has showers. Motels are expensive. If camping, you will be sleeping on permafrost.

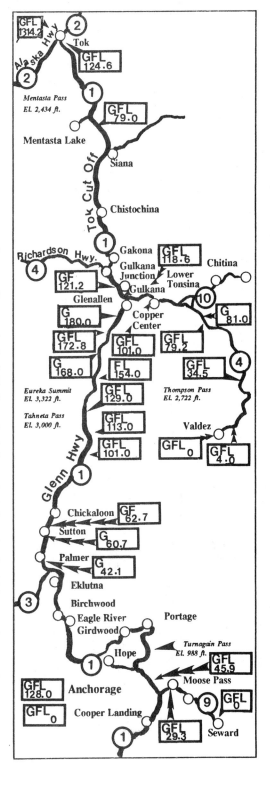

(Top) Off the Sterling Highway to Homer you can ride to the western end of North America, Anchor Point. **(Bottom)** A day-trip out of Anchorage is Homer, 233 miles from Anchorage.

Halibut fishing is what Homer, Alaska, is all about. The town gives birth to some of the world's biggest fish tales and tails. Target the Homer Spit, which extends nearly 5 miles into Homer's Kachemak Bay, for your touristing. There you can camp on the beach, spend $200 a night for a room, hire a charter boat for fishing, shop, and eat some of the best seafood in Alaska. In the summer (high season) the price of housing is so expensive in the Homer area workers on the boats and in the stores/restaurants/hotels sleep in tents on the beach (for a price–camping is not free). The 4.4 mile spit is only 100 yards wide in places and on the weekends jammed with motorhomes, boats and cars. During fishing derby time eagles flying overhead must wonder at the mass of confusion below. For information try the Homer Chamber of Commerce at www.homeralaska.org.

149

CHAPTER 13

ANCHORAGE TO FAIRBANKS

Connected by the George Parks Highway, it is 357 miles between Anchorage and Fairbanks. The biggest attractiion on this highway is Denali National Park, and 20,320-foot-high Mount McKinley. To get into the park, you must leave your motorcycle parked outside the park and take a park bus tour. Camping is available in the park. The bus will drop you off and pick you up at your campground (reservations required). For information on Denali National Park, contact:

Denali National
Park and Preserve
P.O. Box 9
Denali Park, Alaska 99755
Ph. (907) 683-2294
www.nps.gov/dena

Denali National Park is 237 miles north of Anchorage. On a very clear day you can see Mount McKinley from Anchorage. I have seen Mount McKinley only three or four times on my trips to Alaska, as it is often hidden in clouds.

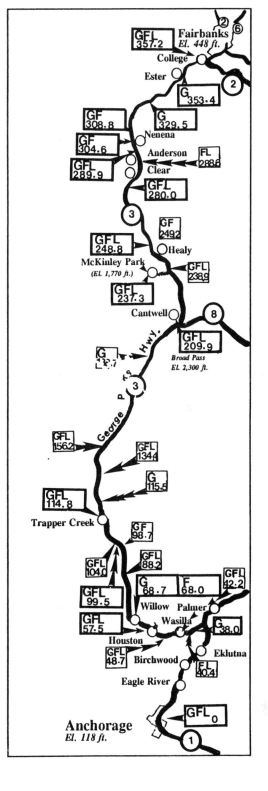

(**Top**) Death is not unknown on the highway to Prudhoe Bay. (**Bottom**) Off into the tundra, a soft mush in summer months. It is best to stay on the gravel road. Here the motorcycle is upright without the help of a center stand . . . stuck in the mush.

CHAPTER 14

TO THE ARCTIC CIRCLE . . . AND BEYOND

From Fairbanks to the Arctic Circle it is an easy day-ride, a round-trip of approximately 400 miles, 250 of which is a gravel road, but well-maintained. In the summer months, there is increasingly more traffic on this road north, as tour buses, motorhomes and family sedans are now making the trip.

The route starts north from Fairbanks on the Steese Highway to Fox, where the Elliott Highway to Manley Hot Springs begins. For the Arctic Circle, follow the Elliott Highway to the junction of the Dalton Highway and then turn north . . . for 126 miles.

The Dalton Highway was built by the Alyeska Pipeline Company in 1974, to haul supplies 414 miles to Prudhoe Bay, thus its nickname, "The Haul Road." Until the mid 1990s, the Dalton Highway was closed to the general public above the Arctic Circle. Adventuresome motorcyclists used to have to wait until the guard at the guard station went home before they could drag their motorcycle under the gate or drive around it, if they wanted to try to reach the Arctic Ocean at Prudhoe Bay. Today, the station is closed and the road is open its entire length.

While any type of motorcycle can travel the length of the Dalton Highway to Prudhoe Bay, and has, something that is comfortable on a gravel road (that can become very greasy with rain) is best. There are some 10% grades, deep ruts and often large (football size) rocks along the way. There is no gas north of Coldfoot, so if the motorcyclist wants to make the ride

(Top) Junction of Elliott Highway and Dalton Highway. From here north, the road is unpaved. **(Bottom)** Watch out for pipeline company trucks from here north.

to Prudhoe Bay they should be able to go 244 miles on their gas supply, or carry extra gas. The road to Five Mile Camp at the Yukon River just below the Arctic Circle has one gas station along the way and there is gas and food at the Yukon River crossing.

At the Arctic Circle, there is a large sign marking the Arctic Circle, as well as a public campground. The road to this point is generally well-maintained, however, numerous motorcyclists have fallen getting to this point, especially if they are not accustomed to traveling on gravel roads. In places, the road is built above the tundra and going off the road means down an embankment sometimes ten feet deep or better. When rain visits the area (possible all summer), the road surface becomes rutted and extremely slippery.

One of my associates, a skilled off-road motorcyclist riding a dual-purpose BMW motorcycle, broke his leg on one of the easier sections of the Dalton Highway. He had been traveling at a normal speed when he went into a section of slippery ruts. His motorcycle, heavy to start with, was packed for camping and the combination of weight and slippery road surface caused him to lose control and ride over the edge. Putting a leg down to try to maintain the motorcycle in an upright position snapped the femur. Fortunately, he was riding with another motorcyclist who was able to keep him from going into shock and get help from Five Mile Camp. The wounded motorcyclist was airlifted by an Army helicopter back to Fairbanks and both he and his motorcycle were shipped back to the Lower 48.

Another one of my riding acquaintances crashed in this same section of road when an approaching truck (it is their road) caused him to get off the smooth section and onto the shoulder. While he suffered only bruises and a deflated ego, his motorcycle was wrecked. It was shipped back to the Lower 48 and he flew home.

These stories make up an average summer on the Dalton Highway. Not only are there crashes (automobiles included), but a minor breakdown can be very costly ($5 per mile, each

From the start of the Dalton Highway to the Arctic Circle sign the Dalton Highway is usually in good condition, unless it is wet. Some is calcium chloride mixed with gravel and can be dusty when dry, very slick when wet!

way, towing charge), as services are limited to the point of being not much more than tundra and rocks.

If the motorcyclist decides to go to Prudhoe Bay (also known as Deadhorse), they will not be able to ride to the Arctic Ocean. Access to the ocean is through the private pipeline company property. At Prudhoe Bay, there are now two bus tours you can take to the water, one a ten-minute ride and a second tour through the pumping facility. Gas, food and lodging are available, but reservations are suggested as more and more tourists are making the trip to Prudhoe each summer.

From Coldfoot north, other than the side road to Wiseman, there are no side trips to be made, and there are no services. The ride is interesting if the weather is good and the road is not wet or snow-covered; otherwise, it can be 244 miles of hell. Before the road was opened all the way to Prudhoe Bay, motorcyclists were an oddity and well-received in Prudhoe Bay. Today the novelty has worn off, as each summer motorcyclists from around the world make the trek north. However, it is the one ride in America where you can say you have ridden "to the end of the earth."

For information, contact:

Alaska Division of Tourism
P.O. Box 110809
Juneau, Alaska 99811
(907) 465-2017
www.dced.state.ak.us/tourism

For information on the pipeline, contact:

Public Affairs
Alyeska Pipeline Service Co.
1835 S. Bragaw St.
Anchorage, Alaska 99512
www.alyeska-pipe.com

Just across the Yukon River, 56 miles from the start of the Dalton Highway, is a gas station and restaurant. The bridge across the Yukon River at this point is wooden and very slippery when wet. There is also a Visitor Center here which is open during the summer. A public campground is nearby.

(**Top**) The Alaska Pipeline runs parallel to the Dalton Highway from Prudhoe Bay. The pipeline is heated so oil can flow through it in the cold weather. Access to the pipeline is closed. (**Bottom**) Nearly any kind of motorcycle can be ridden to the Arctic Circle. Here are Harley Davidsons, BMWs, Honda and a Suzuki, at the Arctic Circle sign.

159

DEADHORSE — PRUDHOE BAY

The ride north from the Arctic Circle sign and campground to Deadhorse becomes a little bit more interesting for the more adventuresome motorcyclist. Fifty miles north of the Arctic Circle is the last gas stop/hotel/restaurant, Coldfoot.

There is not much in Coldfoot and things are expensive. At the one hotel a room runs $100 plus and gas is about 25% more than in Fairbanks. There is no campground in Coldfoot, but for a small fee you can put a tent up between the restaurant and the hotel. From Coldfoot to Deadhorse it is 244 miles, all gravel and mud, depending on the weather.

Once you arrive in Deadhorse (also referred to as Prudhoe Bay) you will find little more than at Coldfoot. Deadhorse has two hotels and a small campground (RV parking). A single room can cost $100 plus (with no TV). A restaurant is available and gas, although expensive, is pumped at the "gas station."

Access to the Arctic Ocean is limited to a bus tour which includes a tour of the oil fields and pumping station. (www.arcticcaribouinn.com). A few lucky individuals have managed to talk their way into the oil fields with their motorcycles and ridden to the Arctic Ocean but this is the exception. A manned gatehouse controls access to the Arctic Ocean/pumping station and seldom do they let motorcyclists through.

Two of my "globetrotting" friends, Susan and Grant Johnson, recently made a run to Deadhorse. Here is what they said of their trip:

"So where the hell is Deadhorse, Alaska, you ask? It's the town that services the Prudhoe Bay oil fields, so it's at the driveable top of North America. Two days up, a day to recuperate, and two days back — about 450 miles each way of poor gravel and dirt roads — the Dalton Highway it's called. The road isn't too bad when it's dry, but very slippery when it's wet, so if it hasn't rained for a few days the highway crews send out water trucks to wet it down just to make it exciting for us motorcyclists! On the way back they didn't need to water the road, the rain got it plenty wet for us. Glad we didn't leave this trip any later. The locals up there say June is spring, July is summer and August is fall."

Any kind of motorcycle can make the trip up to Deadhorse. I have seen Goldwings and heavy weight Harleys make the run. Motorhomes, tour buses and even bicycles regularly make the run to the top. However, a word of caution. If you are not competent in dirt, gravel or mud, you may want to think twice about the last 244 miles. There are plenty of stories about motorcyclists crashing on this section.

The fastest time that I have heard of someone making the run up the Dalton Highway was 8½ hours. In the months of June and July a rider has almost 24 hours of daylight so can expect at least 3/4ths of that to be good enough light to ride comfortably.

However, the last time I went up the Dalton Highway (2003) the weather and road conditions varied considerably. On the lower 100-mile portion there was a forest fire and in places the smoke was so thick I could hardly see the road at 20 miles per hour. At the 150-mile point it started to rain and the unpaved sections up to the Arctic Circle sign were in places as slippery as ice. In the Brooks Range and above, where the road was gravel and normally slippery, it was snowing! That was all in the same day, and a 12-hour period.

One of the smarter riders I met on the Dalton Highway stored all of his heavy gear in Fairbanks at a local motorcycle shop and took only what he needed for one night. He then made the run up to Prudhoe Bay and back in two days, with his motorcycle nearly 100 lbs. lighter. The one thing he did not leave behind was his wet weather riding suit, tent and sleeping bag, all of which he needed when he reached Prudhoe Bay and there were no vacancies and it was raining.

In my 24 trips to and from Alaska since the early 1970s I have seen just about every style of motorcycle, sidecar outfit, trike and trailer combination imaginable in route. I once said the only thing I had not seen was a clown on a unicycle. In 2003 I came close to that combination when I passed the above German man on a stand-up push-bike coming down the Dalton Highway from Deadhorse on his way to the bottom of South America, Ushuaia, Argentina. In my butchered Bavarian and his broken English we agreed that we were having equal fun exploring the wilds of Alaska, although his trepidation level about meeting a bear was much higher than mine.

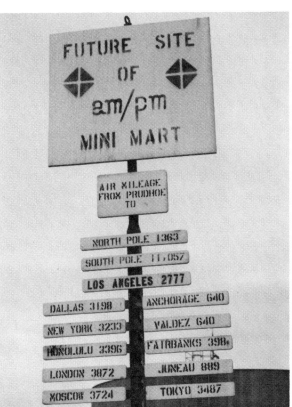

(Top) Mileage home from Deadhorse.
(Bottom) The pumping station, Prudhoe Bay.

159(e)

(Top) The gas station, Prudhoe Bay.
(Bottom) All kinds of vehicles make the run to Prudhoe Bay. This one came from the Mexican border.

159(f)

(Top) One of the two hotels at Prudhoe Bay.
(Bottom) The General Store and post office.

(Thanks to Tom Morgan for this photograph of Slim and his BSA in Fairbanks, Alaska, 1939.)

CHAPTER 15

FROM ALASKA BY MOTORCYCLE – 1939
WITH SLIM WILLIAMS AND JOHN LOGAN

The first motorcyclists to cover much of the ground between Alaska and the Lower 48 were Slim Williams and John Logan. In a 1939 effort to bring attention to the feasibility of a highway between Alaska and the Lower 48, Slim and John rode two BSA single cylinder motorcycles from Fairbanks to Seattle.

Slim Williams, an Alaska sourdough, had previously made the trip by dog sled. John Logan, fresh from Washington and Jefferson College and a short stint in the family hardware business, had made Slim's acquaintance and decided to accept Slim's invitation to ride motorcycles from Alaska. Neither knew how to ride a motorcycle when they started.

After a short section of the Richardson Highway out of Fairbanks, they turned onto trails. Six and one-half months later, they rode into Seattle. Much of their adventure was through mosquito-infested swamps, over game trails and often through wilderness areas where no trails existed. Living off the land, building rafts to get across streams, towing their motorcycle behind a horse for over 100 miles, and carrying their motorcycles in places, these two men were the first motorcyclists to break two-wheeled ground between Alaska and the Lower 48. Much of the route they took six and one-half months to cover in 1939, the modern-day motorcyclist covers in an easy five-day ride.

161

(**Top**) Slim Williams with the two BSA motorcycles and Royal Canadian Mounted Police, 1939. (**Bottom**) Slim Williams crossing rain-swollen river with BSA on self-made log bridge, 1939. (Thanks to Tom Morgan for these photographs.)

I have corresponded with John on several occasions and have found him to be quite unassuming about his adventure sixty years ago. A retired business executive living in Connecticut, he has written about his adventure much the same as he approached the adventure itself, as if it was something to be done. Nowhere in his writings or articles about him or Slim have I come across what would appear to be doubt on their part that their trip could be made. He did say they regretted not switching the motorcycles from battery to magneto ignitions, but even the lack of spark did not deter them from pushing forward with their motorcycles. They managed to solve all mechanical and electrical problems experienced without once visiting a BSA dealer from Dawson City to Vancouver.

John Logan and Slim Williams, a couple of "tough guys," set the record for the longest trip by motorcycle between Alaska and the Lower 48, six and one-half months. Today I believe that if anyone could ride a motorcycle around the moon, my bets would be on John and Slim. The only problem I think they would foresee is how to get both of them and their equipment from here to there.

CHAPTER 16

THE BEAR FACTS

You will be traveling through "bear country," from the Canadian border to the Arctic Circle. Bears can be found just about everywhere, sometimes where you least expect them, like in the city campground rest room.

One of my traveling partners once had a breakdown in Fairbanks that required he stay there until parts could be flown in from Los Angeles. He asked me to call his wife in New York because he said she would not believe him if he told her he was going to have to stay behind for three to five days while the rest of us went ahead. She, being a good New Yorker who only knew of Alaska from TV or movies, took the news that his motorcycle had broken (and would need parts not available in Alaska) in good stride. However, when I told her we were leaving her husband in Fairbanks for a few days her response was quite a bit more concerned. She said, "You mean you are going to leave him there with all those bears?"

I grew up in Montana and while doing so learned a few things about bears. After making over twenty trips to Alaska, I learned a little bit more about bears. Listening to others, I learned even more. While I do not profess to know everything about bears, I can say a few things about bears and motorcyclists:

- Bears remind me of a bumper sticker I have that says, "The more people I meet, the more I like my dog." Bears do not like people.

Potholes in the road are common, and dangerous. Wildlife running across the road in front of you, like deer, caribou, moose and bear, are dangerous. Nothing on your trip north will be as dangerous as a moving vehicle. Assume each one is gong to try and hit you on your motorcycle and you can lower your risk factor. You will be very lucky to see a bear run across the road in front of you.

- On your trip to and from Alaska, your chances of seeing a grizzly or black bear are remote.

- The probability of being injured by a bear is about 1/50th that of being injured in an auto/motorcycle accident on your trip to Alaska.

- Feeding bears is illegal, and hazardous to your health. Ask someone who has been bitten or mauled by one. A bear does not know where the food stops and your hand starts.

- Take pictures of bear with a telephoto lens. I once saw a lady place her child on the back of a bear and wonder why she could not see the child through the Instamatic view finder when she tried to take a picture. The bear had casually dropped the child to the ground and flipped it about 15 feet away with a swipe of its front paw.

- Bears do not like surprises. If you are walking away from camp or anywhere there might be a bear, make noise by whistling or talking to let the bear know you are coming.

- If you do see a bear, leave the area quickly.

- Never run from a bear. Running invites a chase.

- Bears do not have good eyesight. If one stands on its hind legs it is usually trying to determine who, or what, you are. Wave your arms — it might go away, then again it might not.

Moose kicks man to death in Alaska

Associated Press

ANCHORAGE, Alaska — A man was kicked to death at the University of Alaska by a moose that was being harassed by students as it roamed the campus with its calf.

The animals were outside the gym when 71-year-old Myong Chin Ra arrived on Monday to use the sauna. "He tried to just kind of slip by them," said campus police officer Jim Milne, "but that didn't work."

The moose charged, and Ra ran toward a clump of trees. He fell on a slippery walkway, said Shane Harvey, a student. "She'd get on her front legs and kick with her back legs," Harvey said. "He probably got stomped about a dozen times."

(**Top**) Moose are usually timid. Sometimes seen along the roads to Alaska, they seldom run. They can, however, move quickly and errantly. (**Bottom**) This was a nice, photogenic goat, until it started to chew on my motorcycle seat.

- Grizzly bears cannot climb a tree, but they can shake you out of a thin one.

- Black bears are good tree climbers.

- Bears are omnivorous. They will eat almost anything. Do not keep food in your saddlebags, tank bag or around your camp. One evening a bear knocked over six motorcycles while trying to get into a saddlebag which held some sandwich makings. The motorcycles were in the parking lot of a motel.

- Bears are territorial and they will defend their territory, as well as their young.

- Bears are repulsed by the scent of humans.

- The last thing I will say about bears is bears have very differing personalities. They are unpredictable. There are no formulas that apply to all bears.

In my travels to Alaska, I have lost concern of danger from bears. Over the years, I have had a few encounters, some while on the motorcycle and some while off. While they are dangerous, they generally seem to want to be left alone. Usually they go away from me. The two times I have ended up in a tree it was not for long. All the times they came into my camp could have been avoided by first getting the food out of my camp. The biggest danger I worry about traveling by motorcycle is not the bears, nor the moose, it is the motor-homes. They have scared me ever since one made a U-turn in front of a motorcyclist outside of Haines Junction on a straight road. Grampa, driving his first trip to Alaska, said of the motorcyclist who died, "I never saw him."

CHAPTER 17

VISITOR INFORMATION

The following are sources of information along the route to and from Alaska, as well as in Alaska.

ALBERTA

Travel Alberta
6th Floor
Commerce Place
10155 102 St.
Edmonton, AB T5J 4G8 CANADA

BRITISH COLUMBIA

PROVINCE-WIDE
Ministry of Tourism–Dept. T6
Box 9830
STN. PROV. GOVT.
Victoria, BC V8W 9W5 CANADA
1-800-HELLOBC
www.hellobc.com

YUKON

PROVINCE-WIDE
Tourism Yukon, Government of Yukon
P.O. Box 2703
Whitehorse, YT Y1A 2C6 CANADA
(867) 667-5340
www.touryukon.com

ALASKA

STATEWIDE
Alaska Division of Tourism
P.O. Box 110809
Juneau, AK 99811-0809
(907) 465-2017
www.dced.state.ak.us/tourism

Throughout western Canada the roads are well-marked. A free map from the American Automobile Association (if you are a member) should easily get you in, through and out of Canada. While a GPS is a nice gizzmo to add to your motorcycle, it will not be needed.

The one concern some motorcyclists have is the need for a larger gas tank for extra capacity between stations. A 2-3 gallon gas tank will find you dry on certain roads in Canada.

A good used motorcycle coupled with a strong degree of fortitude and the desire to reach faraway places are some of the basic elements needed to ride a motorcycle to Alaska. The rider and his Suzuki pictured above averaged 450 miles per day from California. He made the trip on one set of tires, sprockets and a stock chain. He said that once or twice he had to "manage his speed" to maximize his miles per gallon of gasoline, but never ran dry.

174

THE

ABRIDGED

ALASKA

MOTORCYCLE

ANNALS

The following notes and pictures are from Frazier's photographic and
hand-written diaries after his many travels to and from Alaska.
Some may eventually find their way into his book
MOTORCYCLE ADVENTURER.
Others have all ready found their place in motorcycle print media.
As the editor for this edition of *ALASKA BY MOTORCYCLE,*
I felt the readers might enjoy looking at how "Dr. G"
has seen Alaska on a day to day basis.

"…..on Sunday saw bikini bike wash in Anchorage and stopped to do research for 2nd ed. of MOTORCYCLE SEX book. Girls nice, dancers at Fantasies On 5th Avenue go-go bar. Thought about how I washed the Kawasaki a couple days earlier in a river when a 30-40 lb. salmon swimming upstream knocked me off. Put photos together in something…call Alaska Bike Wash."

"…..10 days and no bears. May go to city dump to get photo, or campground. Plenty of tourist stuff for photos. Totem poles up here are not originally from this area, trees too small. Tourist junk, lot's of tourist junk. No Elvis yet, or Yeti, but saw some crafts made in Bali."

"…Harley shop in Anchorage busy boutique. New HD shop in F'banks empty, but lot's of inventory inside, pretty sales girls both places. Said they sold T-shirts to Harley tourists like ice cubes in Hell."

"*...Kawasaki/BMW shop in Anchorage busy place. Don Rosene, owner, is Indian fan, has at least one. Saw him in Daytona when I was racing my '36 Scout.*"

"*...saw dead BMW on pallet being trucked home. Front wheel folded under engine. Rider error???*"

"Lots of BMWs around. Saw a bunch that came up on the ferry. HD rental shop said a majority of bikes flown up are HDs. HD/BMW rental can run $200-$300/day, and can't take off pavement."

*"Stopped at Anchorage leather shop, 'Don't Ride Naked.'
Owner gone. Saw a mag. on counter with one of my
stories in it. Wanted to meet some naked Alaska girl
riders. No offers."*

   *"...wasn't sure if guy shot the fish or caught it. Said
he'd chased up stream for a mile. Gun on belt was 'fer
bears.' Did have fish pole. Good fish story."*

"Phil Freeman, ALASKA RIDER TOURS.... Runs tours out of Anchorage/ has rental bikes. I called him an 'Alaska Sourdough Motorcyclist.'....we were at the Arctic Circle sign when he caught me putting stickers from Aerostich/RIDERWEARHOUSE on back of sign. Told him I was 'making the scenery more picturesque for the tourists, covering up bullet holes put there by locals.' We're both wearing Aerostich riding gear. Thought he might make me take stickers off. Then I thought I saw his company sticker. He changed subject and moved me away before I could check. Told me to look at the tourist girls getting out of a van that stopped. I'll bet his sticker was there."

"…Dr. John Logan from Lakeland, FL did a field stitch job on Dan Paterno's sliced hand on beer table outside HotSpot motel . I served as nurse…nursed the beer Dan was using for pain. Logan was mc touring with ALASKA RIDER TOURS, had his son as pillion."
"Gas everywhere, but expensive, as always."

"...dual sport bikes had plenty of good off-road riding this summer. Great weather... saw Mt. McKinley three days, twice off-road from backside, Petersville."

"...next summer want to do DEADHORSE ENDURANCE RALLY. www.deadhorserally.com, deadhorserally@yahoo.com. Wonder how many riders crash on Dalton each year? Prudhoe Bay long way."

ARCTIC OCEAN ACCESS RESTRICTIONS

Private vehicles are prohibited on the Prudhoe Bay oil field, which is the only access route to the Arctic Ocean. Access to the oil field and the Arctic Ocean is available only through commercial tours. In Deadhorse, call the Arctic Caribou Inn at 659-2368 or the Prudhoe Bay Hotel at 659-2449.

NEXT SERVICES 240 MILES

James W Dalton Highway

"...restaurants/motels rugged on Dalton Hwy. Not cheap. Hate to be here in winter. I like this part of Alaska best, away from the tourist crowds. 20 years ago I saw no one riding up here, now bikes everywhere."

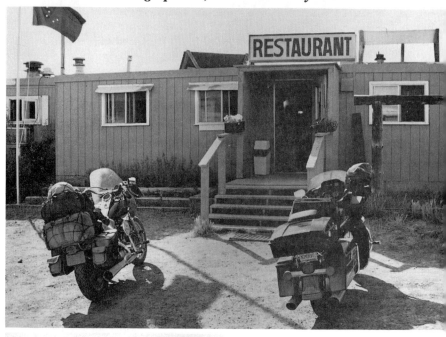

"Ran into a couple BMW guys today. Guy on old K100RS bought bike cheap, rode to Alaska, swapped tires in Fairbanks, bought cheap plastic gas can and did Deadhorse up/back in two days. Other guy had gizzmo's and 5 times as much in bike. Both had same fun."

"Forest fire on Dalton near Livingood, rain at Arctic Circle and Coldfoot, snow 50 miles north in Brooks Range...all same day, July. God/Buddha/Nature!"

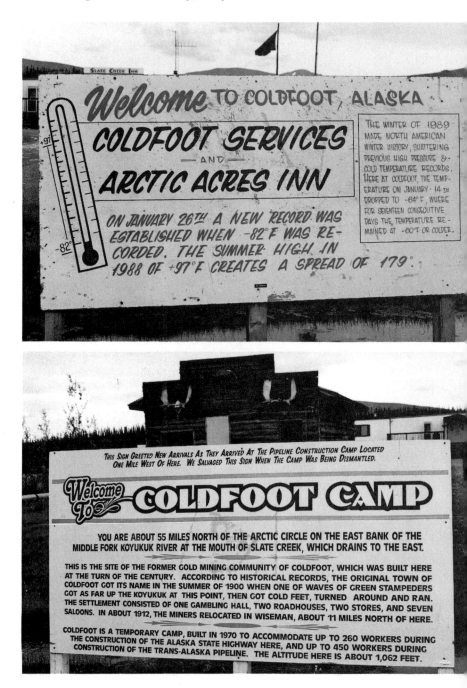

ALASKA OFF THE ROAD

(First published in DUAL SPORT NEWS)

Bears, mud, gravel, tundra, snow, ice, fire, and fun. Throw in a motorcycle that is manageable both on and off-road, then pick a summer month, and you can find yourself in Alaska.

The trick to off-road adventure in Alaska is putting the pieces together.

Alaska is a long distance from anywhere in the "Lower 48." A gentle ride to "America's Last Frontier" can take from a week to 10 days, one way. If you are looking for off-road riding after you have ridden to the Land of The Midnight Sun, that means you have probably chewed up a pair of tires and may be well through a set of sprockets and a chain. You have to figure the same to get back home.

Once you arrive in Alaska you are going to find that for a state as huge as it is, Alaska does not offer a proportionate amount of off-road riding. One reason is that small airplanes do most treks into the wilderness. Another is that once you venture off the main roads in the summer you will likely find yourself wallowing through black mud, which is what tundra becomes in the summer when it warms up.

There are a number of gravel roads that cut through Alaska's wilderness; the trick is to find them, and to do so when passable. Where and when they are doable you should not be surprised to see almost any kind of motorcycle crossing them, especially in the summer. Most of the gravel roads are good enough for 18-wheelers, which is why they were probably built in the first place, to haul goods in and out of the wilderness, like supplies to pumping stations along the Alyeska Pipeline.

The best riding months are June-August, although there are no guarantees that you won't ride through rain, snow or ice in this period. On the other hand, there is a possibility that forest fires may close a road if the smoke is thick enough during the same week it snows.

RENT AND RIDE

Short on time and money? An option is to fly to Anchorage and take a guided tour or rent a dual-sport bike and do your own exploring. For what it would cost to ride your own bike to Alaska you can fly and ride for nearly the same price, and instead of spending two weeks getting to and from Alaska you can spend that time adventuring in Alaska. The wrinkle is to find the dual-sport niche, and a motorcycle on which to do it.

Several motorcycle rent-al agencies in Alaska have a clause in their rental agreements prohibiting off-pavement use (especially heavyweight bike rentals). Another says "No!" to a run up to Prudhoe Bay on the Dalton Highway, which is about two-thirds gravel.

One company, Alaska Rider Tours, offers both off-road rentals and guided off-road tours, a unique option for the adventure rider.

The off-road guided tour includes a run to the Arctic Circle, coupled with several days of rough riding over gravel roads. While not required to ride in a group following the group leader at a sedate pace, this gaggle option is available for the meek and mild. However, if the group wants to try the rough stuff, owner/operator Phil Freeman was quick to change the dance floor. The more adventuresome could strike out on their own for the day, rendezvousing at night at the designated motel, bed and breakfast or campground. During the day a shag wagon ferried luggage, tents, food and even a spare dual-sport bike to the evenings resting point.

This was definitely not one of the slick tours promoted by tour companies catering to the fat cats spreading American Express charge slips around lounges at Marriott Hotels, bragging about how they and their rented Harley had conquered 200 miles of the paved and trailer clogged Alaska Highway. Instead, each day the riders found themselves well away from the flocks of tourists that poured out of RVs, buses and station wagons jammed with screaming kids. Imagine yourself 40 miles off the paved highway, crossing a glacial stream with 400-lb. bears slapping spawning salmon onto the shore on each side for their noon day meal. Or a moose wandering through your campsite at night. How about picturing yourself at the Arctic Circle sign after having ridden through a forest fire to get there? An off-road guided tour can put you in those pictures.

OFF THE PAVED ROADS

Pull out a map of Alaska and look at the roads. The system is pretty much a circle around the inner part of the state with some paved road as offshoots to points like Homer and Valdez, where you have to turn around and ride back. A little closer inspection shows there are some gravel roads, like the Top Of The World Highway through Chicken to Dawson City, or the Denali Highway. These are good, high speed gravel roads, but often you will find wallowing motor homes or tour buses filled with senior citizens in your way, especially at the restaurants or scenic turn outs for photographs.

Look a little closer at the map and you will see some dotted lines going into wilderness areas. These are less traveled and often lead to gold mines, and they are the ones that dual-sport motorcycles are made for hammering. If you have ridden your bike from the Lower 48 you will most likely find yourself overloaded for these roads, and opting to stick with the Alaska Tourist Trail (RV passable roads). However, these little roads/trails are what you will need to ride if you want to get a taste of what Alaska wilderness really is,

those like you see in the National Geographic.

THE QUICKIE RUN

The Dalton Highway runs to the furthest point north on the North American continent you can ride/drive a vehicle. For the first 100 miles the surface is mixed, some paved, some gravel. From Coldfoot (the last gas) to Deadhorse (also known as Prudhoe Bay) the road can be high-speed gravel or rocks/mud/snow/ rain/and ice from your worst nightmare, and that can be in July! It depends on the fickle Alaska weather. You have to cross the Brooks Mountain Range, and while one year to forest below the Arctic Circle was on fire, there was ice and blowing snow in the Brooks Range.

It is not unheard of for a rider to make the run from Fairbanks to Deadhorse in one day, then back down the next. Other stories abound about taking 10-20 hours merely to make the run from Coldfoot to Deadhorse, only 242 miles. The current "high-water" time for the fastest one way run is about 8 ½ hours from the start to the top, but that was on a friendly weather day.

If you have limited time and a tight schedule, the quick run "off the paved roads" is up to Deadhorse and back. Plan on two long days, and also plan on riding 600 miles of gravel that can turn to iced glass if it rains and gets cool.

THINGS I TOOK:

I used a stock Kawasaki KLR 650 from Alaska Rider Tours. Knowing I was going to be sitting on a factory seat for 10-12 hours per day, I decided to take a bum-helper in the form of an Aerostitch Sheepskin Saddle Pad, a wise decision. (www.aerostitch.com) To fight the wind and rain I bolted on an 11-inch high windshield from Clearview Shields. (www.clearviewshields.com)

For day luggage (spare tubes, cameras, rain gear, water and tools) I added my own tankbag and panniers from Dual-Star that was designed specifically for the KLR gas tank. (www.dual-star.com)

I wanted to try some saddlebags on the back, but nothing too expensive, so bolted on a set of Dirt-Bagz by Moto-Sport Panniers. (www.dirt-bagz.com)

For rain, which I counted on, and experienced, I was overly pleased with the Aerostitch Triple Digit Rain Cover Gloves and Ultralight Rain Pants. Both took nearly no space and kept the water out when it came down. I also used their Kanetsu Electric Liner for the days it rained and at nights for a pillow. (www.aerostitch.com)

ALASKA ADVENTURE

(Published in
MOTORCYCLE
CONSUMER NEWS, January
2004)

Alaska by motorcycle equals riding to Earth's End. A little known fact is that Alaska offers motorcyclists two opportunities to reach riding goals. The first is to ride to the furthest highway point west on the North American Continent, Anchor Point. The second is the furthest point north, Prudhoe Bay, also known as Deadhorse.

Alaska also means bears, mountains, glaciers, fish, tundra, ice, snow, mosquitoes, the "midnight sun" and America's "Last Frontier." The choices for the motorcyclist are how much time and money to budget, when to go, what bike to take, and how to get there.

How Long and How Far and How Much Money

From Seattle, Washington to Anchorage, Alaska, by the most direct road route, is 2,435 miles. For the big rider that is a couple of long days. For the average motorcyclist it is about a week.

Once in Alaska a minimum stay should be five to seven days to do the high point tourist things. Then it is another week back to the "Lower 48." Add in a couple of days for laundry, Internet, tire/oil change, resting, touristing and your plan should be for three weeks.

Depending from where you began your ride, up and back can be anywhere from 5,000 to 10,000 miles.

Starting from a base of $100.00 per day for food, gas, oil, and sleeping you budget base would be approximately $2,000.00 and that is doing some sleeping on the ground. It is not unusual to spend twice that per day (a "cheap" room in Anchorage was $80.00 in 2003 while the Holiday Inn quoted something closer to $200.00 per night) if eating and sleeping high end. Throw in a set of tires, some swill at night, new riding suit and helmet, waterproof gloves, a GPS, larger gas tank, cold weather sleeping bag, chain and sprockets, Canadian and travel insurance, and now your starting to hammer the credit card pretty hard, easily between $6,000.00 and $10,000.00.

When To Go

June through August provide the best window for riding in the North, those being the warmest months, but often the wettest. Anchorage's heaviest rain period is August and September. 358 miles away in Fairbanks July and August is the rainy season.

On July 2, 2003, the Dalton Highway, 84 miles north of Fairbanks was closed due to smoke from forest fires burning along the road. Six hours north, in the Brooks Mountain Range, the road was nearly impassable due to snow!

June 21 (summer solstice) provides 19 hours and 21 minutes of daylight in Anchorage. Neighboring Fairbanks has more than 21 hours of daylight the same day. These long daylight hours allow for long riding days.

The downside to riding to Alaska in this three month window is the highways, hotels, campgrounds and gas stations are often clogged with tourists, RVs, and wallowing tour buses. If your plans include sleeping indoors make your reservations months in advance or you may find no room at the inn.

What Bike To Ride

The image of some motorcyclist flogging an overloaded motorcycle with spare tires strapped to the back through foot deep mud ruts up the Alaska Highway is history. So is the need for huge aftermarket gas tanks, knobby tires and suicide pills in case you are attacked by a rabid bear and left for dead.

Each summer motorhomes and 1,000's of trailers are towed up and down the Alaska Highway to Anchorage. One of the largest Airstream trailer conventions in North America was held in Anchorage, most of them having been towed there.

What this means is the Alaska Highway (and soon the Cassiar Highway) is paved the entire distance. The unpaved sections are those being repaired, and ongoing process due to breakage caused by freezing.

Translated to motorcycles this means that anything from 2000-cc to 50-cc models can be ridden to and from Alaska. There is no need to purchase a special purpose enduro type motorcycle and equip it for a 'round the world ride just for a run to Alaska. Gas is plentiful and frequent (although pricey in places), restaurants with "good home cooking" evenly spaced, and hotels/motels/campgrounds easy jumping distance for the poseur adventurer.

The recommended motorcycle is something that is comfortable to sit on for long riding days, preferably with some windscreen up front (for rain, bugs, flying stones, and cold air). Carrying capacity is a personal choice. One sport bike rider from Los Angeles opted for a tank bag on the front and sleeping bag on the back. Another chose to take the sidecar (for the wife) with trailer on the back ("for souvenirs"). Both successfully negotiated the infamous Alaska Highway up and back.

How To Reach Alaska

Riding up and back takes time. Mistakenly many riders assume they will have to ride the same road (The Alaska Highway) up and back, therefore making the second leg boring. An option is the Cassiar Highway (there is about 100 miles of high speed gravel, with trailers being towed), possibly the most picturesque ride to Alaska, inland through British Colombia. With a little planning and grit a rider can

vector over the Top of The World Highway to Dawson City, then through Ross River to Watson Lake, and do less than 50 miles of the Alaska Highway twice, all in about the same time as riding up and down the Alaska Highway takes.

Many motorcyclists (100's each summer) choose to take the ferryboat from Bellingham, Washington to Haines, Alaska, suggesting they are saving time by doing so.

The ferryboat ride takes four nights. With the long daylight hours and routing up the Cassiar Highway, road riders arrive at Haines Junction at nearly the same time as the boat people. The price to ride to boat starts (in 2003) at $359.00 for the motorcycle (under 10 feet in length) and $287.00 per person (that is sleeping on the deck). For a low cost cabin (with two bunks) add $276.00 (1 person or 2). Meals are extra.

The ferryboat leaves twice a week, so some scheduling comes into play. On the upside many riders argue that when they reach Alaska they have not worn our tires, chains, sprockets and themselves, a valid argument. This can translate into cash savings if tires, chains or sprockets have to be changed on the road, oftentimes a time-consuming (items may have to be ordered and flown in) and expensive adventure in Anchorage, Fairbanks or Whitehorse.

Another option is to have your motorcycle shipped by boat into Anchorage from Seattle (or other points via Seattle). A "one stop" service out of Seattle to Anchorage charges $175.00 for receiving and crating your motorcycle, and $25.00 for delivery to the shipping company. Once there it is placed in a container and ten days later arrives in Anchorage for between $300.00-$400.00. A logistical wrinkle for this option is the boats leave Seattle on Wednesday or Friday, therein requiring an arrival several days earlier.

Shipping by air from Seattle to Anchorage by air cargo is also possible, but limited by the number of air cargo carriers that will carry motorcycles, which are classified as Dangerous Goods. One air cargo company quoted a price of $.61/lb., uncrated, but said delivery would be on a "space available" basis, which means it may or may not go out of Seattle on the day promised. A word of caution on shipping by air: the Captain is God. This means that as he is walking around and inspecting the goods to be loaded onto his plane and sees a motorcycle, with empty gas tank, and battery removed, he can easily say "No" to its being loaded.

Rental motorcycles are available in Alaska, something new in the last several years. Several companies are based in Anchorage. One offered Harley-Davidsons for a daily rate of $190.00. A second company had an array of late model BMW's for rent ranging from $89.00 for a F650 to $170.00 for a R1150GSA. A third agency offered enduro models (Suzuki DRs and Kawasaki KLRs) for $100.00 per day. All offered discounts for long term rentals. A fourth option for HOG members is a HOG rental through one of the Harley-Davidson dealers in Alaska.

Finally there is the option of flying into Alaska and signing up for one of several full package tours. These range in price and duration and include guides, some meals, varied accommodations, options on makes and models of motorcycles and shag wagons to carry luggage and spare parts. One of the least expensive (and shorter duration) tours was around the $3,000.00 mark for 6 nights, which included airport pick-up and drop-off, moderate to high end hotels/B&B's, three nights camping and all dinners and breakfasts.

Bears

One of the most often asked questions is "What about the bears?" While stories abound about motorcyclists running into bears or being chased by them, the truth is you are probably not going to see a bear unless you go looking for one. The odds are much higher of running into a moose, and generally they do not chase motorcyclists. If one does, you will have had a real Alaska adventure.

****

Rental Companies

Alaska Motorcycle
Adventures
(907) 376-4514
www.rentalaska.com
Alaska Rider Tours
(800) 756-1990
www.akrider.com

Motorcycle Shipping

KGM Assemblers
(800) 378-6618

JC Motors
(800) 730-3151

Alaska Classic Motion
(From Alaska)
(907) 272-6863
www.classicmotionak.com

Alaska Tour Companies

Alaska Rider Tours
(800) 756-1990
www.akrider.com

Edelweiss Bike Travel
(800) 507-4459
www.edelweissbike.com

Arctic Motorcycle
Tours and Rentals
(Based in Canada)
(867) 633-3344
www.arcticmoto.com

THE ROAD TO DEADHORSE

(Published in RIDER Magazine, 2005)

Mental medicine or mettle madness, riding over Gobblers Knob to Deadhorse? Loss of cell phone connect along the way for some trepid riders may equal stepping off the end of the earth, which they can physically do when they reach the end of this road. For others, reaching Deadhorse can equate to blissful hours of two-wheel solitude.

To intrepid motorcycle adventure seekers and long distance riders, tagging the furthest point north on the North American continent means a run up the Dalton Highway to Prudhoe Bay, Alaska. Long known as one of America's most remote and challenging roads, these 414 miles can humble those who think they, and their motorcycle manufacturers, know something about hard rides. For others, the test of surviving extreme weather conditions, treacherous road surfaces, wild animals and "No Services" is the mental satisfaction they are rewarded with for their preparedness.

The Dalton Highway was built to haul supplies to and from Prudhoe Bay after oil was discovered there in 1969. Constructed in 1974, the completion in five months was an engineering feat that balanced that of the parallel construction of the Alyeska Pipeline along which the road runs. The main wells and pumping station at Prudhoe Bay needed everything from people to pipe in a rush to solve an energy crisis and move the black gold from the Arctic Slope to the Alaska port of Valdez, 800 miles south.

Building the major section between the Yukon River, 140 miles from Fairbanks, and Prudhoe Bay meant crossing not only the Arctic Circle, but also hundreds of miles of tundra that became a mud bog in summer and one of the coldest places in North America during the winter. Thrown in was having to traverse the Brooks Mountain Range

ORDER FORM

Whole Earth Motorcycle Center
P.O. Box 102125
Denver, Colorado 80250-2125

Please send me the following:

_____ copies of *ALASKA BY MOTORCYCLE* @ $19.95 plus $5.00 shipping and handling.

NAME _____

ADDRESS _____

_____

CITY, STATE, ZIP _____

I understand that I may return any book for a full refund if not satisfied.

Shipping Charges. Please add $5.00 for the first book and $1.00 for any additional book ordered.

MOTORCYCLE

SEX

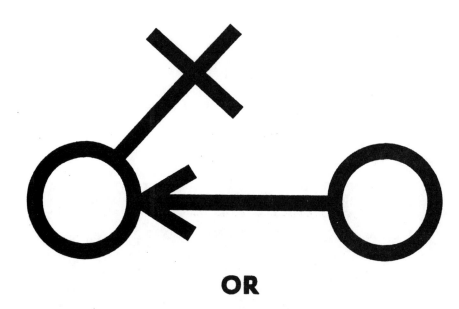

OR

FREUD WOULD NEVER UNDERSTAND THE RELATIONSHIP BETWEEN ME AND MY MOTORCYCLE.

MOTORCYCLE SEX OR: FREUD WOULD NEVER UNDERSTAND THE RELATIONSHIP BETWEEN ME AND MY MOTORCYCLE

A motorcyclist's analysis of the Freudian analysts.

MOTORCYCLE ·SEX **includes:**

- Daimler versus Freud: The theory of problem solving
- Dispelling "Kentucky Fried Freud" in America
- Motorcycles are erotic, not psychotic
- Waylon Barstow's *"Biker Love Chant"*
- Naked Ladies and motorcycles
- Orgasmic Roads in America
- Snakes and riding naked
- Motorcycle racing — bungee jumping without a bungee
- Comical anecdotes reveal Sigmund Freud's failures in the motorcycle world

Self-love and sex were defined by Freud as narcissism. Object-choice is often confused with narcissistic identification. The choice between a motorcycle and a human being is a cathexis incomprehensible to Freud, being neither narcissistic/self-love or object-choice. It is merely a cathect of a sexual object. *MOTORCYCLE SEX* can be a nightmare for 200,000 Freudian therapists in America.

MOTORCYCLE SEX:	150 pages
ISBN:	0-935151-19-2
PRICE:	$19.95 plus $5.00 shipping and handling
FROM:	Whole Earth Motorcycle Center
	P.O. Box 102125
	Denver, CO 80250-2125 USA
	VISA/MASTERCARD 1-800-532-5557

Dr. Gregory W. Frazier

RIDING
SOUTH

*Mexico, Central America
and South America
by Motorcycle*

*Motorcycle Adventurer's
Handbook*

Motorcycle to the "end of the earth." Ride through Mexico, Central America and South America with professional motorcycle adventurer Dr. Gregory Frazier. 31,000 miles across hostile borders, through snake infested jungles, over arid deserts and the glacier fields of Patagonia.

If you have ever dreamed of making a motorcycle ride to places like the Copper Canyon in Mexico (wider, deeper and seven times larger than the Grand Canyon), Peru's sacred Machu Picchu, the jungles of the Amazon or Tierra del Fuego (the "Land of Fire"), the southern most reachable point in South America, **RIDING SOUTH** shows you how to make your dream come true.

RIDING SOUTH has answers to hundreds of questions regarding motorcycle travel in Latin America. It can save you hundreds to thousands of dollars if you are budget conscious. It can also save you from making costly mistakes concerning choice of motorcycles and traveling gear.

RIDING SOUTH, the only publication of its kind in the world, is an absolute must for the motorcyclist with dreams of riding south of America's border towards the end of the earth.

ARROWSTAR PUBLISHING

$24.95

Dr. Gregory W. Frazier

New Zealand
by Motorcycle

*A "Motorcycle Friendly"
handbook for two wheel
travelers and adventurers.*

Motorcycle Adventurer's
Handbook

New Zealand by Motorcycle

Kiwis, penguins, beaches, jungles, Southern Alps, volcanoes, and perfect motorcycling roads are all found in New Zealand. Considered by many motorcyclists to be the "ultimate motorcycling destination," New Zealand is a motorcycle dream ride. Dr. Gregory W. Frazier, America's foremost motorcycling adventure author (ALASKA BY MOTORCYCLE, EUROPE BY MOTORCYCLE, MEXICO, CENTRAL AMERICA AND SOUTH AMERICA BY MOTORCYCLE) passes on his wealth of New Zealand motorcycling knowledge in NEW ZEALAND BY MOTORCYCLE.

Subjects covered include:

- *A guided tour versus independent travel*
- *The best motorcycling roads*
- *Paperwork requirements*
- *Contacts for motorcyclists*
- *Planning tips and timesavers*
- *Budget considerations*
- *Motorcycle travel tips and advice*

ISBN 0-935151-22-2

51995

9 780935 151220

A "Motorcycle Friendly" handbook for two wheel travelers and adventurers.

ARROWSTAR PUBLISHING
$19.95

**Alpine Adventure Films
Presents**

MOTORCYCLING ON THE TEN BEST HIGHWAYS IN AMERICA

MOTORCYCLING IN AMERICA

"MOTORCYCLING ON THE TEN BEST HIGHWAYS IN AMERICA" is a video "riders manual" on motorcycling on the best motorcycling roads in America. Included is information on where the best roads are, when they are open, riding conditions and tips for enjoying these roads on a motorcycle.

Whole Earth Motorcycle Center, P.O. Box 102125, Denver, CO 80250-2125

"MOTORCYCLING ON THE TEN BEST HIGHWAYS IN AMERICA" is a unique motorcycling documentary about motorcycling on the best roadways in America. Scripted and researched by motorcyclists, this film gives the viewer a taste of each of the ten best motorcycling roads in America. Filmed from motorcycles, this video is the nearest thing to actually riding these great American roads. The video includes maps and riding tips, as well as secrets for enjoying motorcycling at its best.

"MOTORCYCLING ON THE TEN BEST HIGHWAYS IN AMERICA" is a video travel adventure and a requirement for the complete motorcycle video library collection.

To order *"MOTORCYCLING ON THE TEN BEST HIGHWAYS IN AMERICA"* send check or money order for $24.95 plus $5.00 shipping and handling to: Whole Earth Motorcycle Center, P.O. Box 102125, Denver, CO 80250-2125. Mastercard and VISA orders call the 800 order line at 1-800-532-5557.

TWO WHEEL WANDERLUST

TRAVELING AROUND THE WORLD BY MOTORCYCLE

"TWO WHEEL WANDERLUST: TRAVELING AROUND THE WORLD BY MOTORCYCLE"

is the first video documentary ever produced on travel by motorcycle around the world.

What makes a person yearn for a motorcycle trip around the earth? How long should one plan for a "global ride?" Should the dream ride be solo or in the company of another adventurer? What about security, border crossings, health concerns, motorcycle preparation and which motorcycle to take? How much does a world tour cost? What about a "safety net" while the thrill seeker is on the road?

"TWO WHEEL WANDERLUST" includes interviews with global road warriors and Guinness record holders Dave Barr (first man around the world on a Harley Davidson) and Nick Sanders (fastest man around the world on a motorcycle).

Narrated by Dr. Gregory W. Frazier, America's foremost motorcycle adventure journalist/author and twice "around the globe" by motorcycle rider, this film answers many of the questions raised by motorcyclists dreaming of a ride around the world.

60 minutes in length, **"TWO WHEEL WANDERLUST"** includes colorful interviews, rare international travel footage and numerous tips on global travel.

ABOUT THE AUTHOR

Professional motorcycle adventurer Dr. Gregory W. Frazier is the only known motorcyclist to have made four circumnavigations of the world, literally riding motorcycles "to the ends of the earth." His adventures include having to dismantle his motorcycle and carry it over a 13,000-foot-high Rocky Mountain pass, building a raft from logs and floating his bike with luggage across a rain-swollen stream, and being shot at by rebels while traveling through an unfriendly country. About his adventures he says, "*I hate any adventure that involves sharks or snakes.*"

Dr. Frazier is a well-known motorcycle journalist whose work has appeared in motorcycle publications throughout the world. He has written numerous motorcycle travel books that have received wide acclaim, including **NEW ZEALAND BY MOTORCYCLE**; **RIDING SOUTH: Mexico, Central America and South America by Motorcycle**; **EUROPE BY MOTORCYCLE** and **BMW GSing AROUND THE WORLD**. Frazier has also produced nearly a dozen motorcycle documentary films.

A veteran of over 24 trips to and from Alaska, including several while a motorcycle tour guide, Frazier is an acknowledged expert on motorcycling to and from America's Last Frontier.

When not adventuring around the world Dr. Frazier lives on his ranch in the Big Horn Mountains of Montana. Part Crow Indian, he attributes much of his two-wheel wanderlust to his American Indian heritage. He is single with no dependents, other than his motorcycles.

Many of Frazier's motorcycle adventures can be followed on his website at:

www.horizonsunlimited.com/gregfrazier

Marilyn Reno
Editor

FROM THE EDITOR

This edition of **ALASKA BY MOTOR-CYCLE** will be updated as future editions are published. If you have items you think should be included, let us know. If you have photographs you believe would be interesting to future adventurers, send them along.

We want to try and keep **ALASKA BY MOTORCYCLE** as current as possible so future motorcyclists can benefit from other motorcyclists' adventures.

Send information to:

ARROWSTAR PUBLISHING
Attn: **ALASKA BY MOTORCYCLE**
P.O. Box 100134
Denver, CO 80250-0134